THE EFFECT OF TELEVISION VIOLENCE ON CHILDREN: WHAT POLICYMAKERS NEED TO KNOW

United States Congress House of Representatives Committee on Energy and Commerce, Subcommittee on Telecommunications and the Internet

The BiblioGov Project is an effort to expand awareness of the public documents and records of the U.S. Government via print publications. In broadening the public understanding of government and its work, an enlightened democracy can grow and prosper. Ranging from historic Congressional Bills to the most recent Budget of the United States Government, the BiblioGov Project spans a wealth of government information. These works are now made available through an environmentally friendly, print-on-demand basis, using only what is necessary to meet the required demands of an interested public. We invite you to learn of the records of the U.S. Government, heightening the knowledge and debate that can lead from such publications.

UNIVERSITY OF CHICHESTER

Included are the following Collections:

Budget of The United States Government	Code of Federal Regulations
Presidential Documents	Congressional Documents
United States Code	Economic Indicators
Education Reports from ERIC	Federal Register
GAO Reports	Government Manuals
History of Bills	House Journal
House Rules and Manual	Privacy act Issuances
Public and Private Laws	Statutes at Large

THE EFFECT OF TELEVISION VIOLENCE ON CHILDREN: WHAT POLICYMAKERS NEED TO KNOW

HEARING

BEFORE THE

SUBCOMMITTEE ON TELECOMMUNICATIONS AND THE INTERNET

OF THE

COMMITTEE ON ENERGY AND COMMERCE

HOUSE OF REPRESENTATIVES

ONE HUNDRED EIGHTH CONGRESS

SECOND SESSION

SEPTEMBER 13, 2004

Serial No. 108–116

Printed for the use of the Committee on Energy and Commerce

Available via the World Wide Web: http://www.access.gpo.gov/congress/house

U.S. GOVERNMENT PRINTING OFFICE

96–095PDF   WASHINGTON : 2004

For sale by the Superintendent of Documents, U.S. Government Printing Office
Internet: bookstore.gpo.gov   Phone: toll free (866) 512–1800; DC area (202) 512–1800
Fax: (202) 512–2250   Mail: Stop SSOP, Washington, DC 20402–0001

COMMITTEE ON ENERGY AND COMMERCE

JOE BARTON, Texas, *Chairman*

W.J. "BILLY" TAUZIN, Louisiana
RALPH M. HALL, Texas
MICHAEL BILIRAKIS, Florida
FRED UPTON, Michigan
CLIFF STEARNS, Florida
PAUL E. GILLMOR, Ohio
JAMES C. GREENWOOD, Pennsylvania
CHRISTOPHER COX, California
NATHAN DEAL, Georgia
RICHARD BURR, North Carolina
ED WHITFIELD, Kentucky
CHARLIE NORWOOD, Georgia
BARBARA CUBIN, Wyoming
JOHN SHIMKUS, Illinois
HEATHER WILSON, New Mexico
JOHN B. SHADEGG, Arizona
CHARLES W. "CHIP" PICKERING,
   Mississippi, *Vice Chairman*
VITO FOSSELLA, New York
STEVE BUYER, Indiana
GEORGE RADANOVICH, California
CHARLES F. BASS, New Hampshire
JOSEPH R. PITTS, Pennsylvania
MARY BONO, California
GREG WALDEN, Oregon
LEE TERRY, Nebraska
MIKE FERGUSON, New Jersey
MIKE ROGERS, Michigan
DARRELL E. ISSA, California
C.L. "BUTCH" OTTER, Idaho
JOHN SULLIVAN, Oklahoma

JOHN D. DINGELL, Michigan
   Ranking Member
HENRY A. WAXMAN, California
EDWARD J. MARKEY, Massachusetts
RICK BOUCHER, Virginia
EDOLPHUS TOWNS, New York
FRANK PALLONE, Jr., New Jersey
SHERROD BROWN, Ohio
BART GORDON, Tennessee
PETER DEUTSCH, Florida
BOBBY L. RUSH, Illinois
ANNA G. ESHOO, California
BART STUPAK, Michigan
ELIOT L. ENGEL, New York
ALBERT R. WYNN, Maryland
GENE GREEN, Texas
KAREN McCARTHY, Missouri
TED STRICKLAND, Ohio
DIANA DeGETTE, Colorado
LOIS CAPPS, California
MICHAEL F. DOYLE, Pennsylvania
CHRISTOPHER JOHN, Louisiana
TOM ALLEN, Maine
JIM DAVIS, Florida
JANICE D. SCHAKOWSKY, Illinois
HILDA L. SOLIS, California
CHARLES A. GONZALEZ, Texas

BUD ALBRIGHT, *Staff Director*
JAMES D. BARNETTE, *General Counsel*
REID P.F. STUNTZ, *Minority Staff Director and Chief Counsel*

SUBCOMMITTEE ON TELECOMMUNICATIONS AND THE INTERNET

FRED UPTON, Michigan, *Chairman*

MICHAEL BILIRAKIS, Florida
CLIFF STEARNS, Florida
   Vice Chairman
PAUL E. GILLMOR, Ohio
CHRISTOPHER COX, California
NATHAN DEAL, Georgia
ED WHITFIELD, Kentucky
BARBARA CUBIN, Wyoming
JOHN SHIMKUS, Illinois
HEATHER WILSON, New Mexico
CHARLES W. "CHIP" PICKERING,
   Mississippi
VITO FOSSELLA, New York
STEVE BUYER, Indiana
CHARLES F. BASS, New Hampshire
MARY BONO, California
GREG WALDEN, Oregon
LEE TERRY, Nebraska
JOE BARTON, Texas,
   (Ex Officio)

EDWARD J. MARKEY, Massachusetts
   Ranking Member
ALBERT R. WYNN, Maryland
KAREN McCARTHY, Missouri
MICHAEL F. DOYLE, Pennsylvania
JIM DAVIS, Florida
CHARLES A. GONZALEZ, Texas
RICK BOUCHER, Virginia
EDOLPHUS TOWNS, New York
BART GORDON, Tennessee
PETER DEUTSCH, Florida
BOBBY L. RUSH, Illinois
ANNA G. ESHOO, California
BART STUPAK, Michigan
ELIOT L. ENGEL, New York
JOHN D. DINGELL, Michigan,
   (Ex Officio)

(II)

CONTENTS

THE EFFECT OF TELEVISION VIOLENCE ON CHILDREN: WHAT POLICYMAKERS NEED TO KNOW

MONDAY, SEPTEMBER 13, 2004

House of Representatives,
Committee on Energy and Commerce,
Subcommittee on Telecommunications
and the Internet,
Chicago, IL.

The subcommittee met, pursuant to notice, at 9:30 a.m., Neal F. Simeon Career Academy, 8147 South Vincennes Avenue, Chicago, Illinois, Hon. Fred Upton (chairman) presiding.

Members present: Representatives Upton, Shimkus and Rush.

Staff present: Kelly Cole, majorty counsel; Will Norwind, majority counsel and policy coordinator; Howard Waltzman, majority counsel; Andy Black, deputy staff director; and Peter Filon, minority counsel.

STATEMENT OF JOHN EVERETT, PRINCIPAL, NEAL F. SIMEON CAREER ACADEMY

Mr. EVERETT. Let me have your attention for a minute, please. First, I'd like to welcome my distinguished guests. And I say good morning to my favorite students. It's really a pleasure to have affair of this magnitude here at Simeon. We had a groundbreaking ceremony, I mean a rivetting-breaking ceremony last year at this time. And we had the Mayor out, and we had all the dignitaries. And now we have our favorite Congressman, Bobby Rush, and some more dignitaries out.

So, Simeon is known to have dignitaries. But let me say that this is a real, real educational experience for our students. They don't have civics, per se in the high schools anymore. But this is a true, true civics lesson. So, please enjoy yourself and learn something from this. Because this is what it's all about. Thank you, and let's have a good day. Thanks.

Mr. UPTON. Well, thank you very much. My name is Fred Upton. I'm a Congressman from across Lake Michigan, in St. Joe/Benton Harbor. And the first thing that I noticed when I walked in the school was the name Wolverine. I am a Wolverine, I just wanted you to know. And I know our Wolverines here and in Michigan took a tough loss on Saturday. But with all of that, I know that there will be a better week next week. But good morning, today's hearing is entitled "The Effect of Television Violence on Children: What Policymakers Need to Know."

I'm honored to be here today with my good friend Bobby Rush, in his district, and I am pleased that John Shimkus, another Congressman from downstate Illinois, is with us today as well. I want to thank the administrators, faculty, and especially the students, you all, of this academy, for help hosting us here this morning. And just so that we are all on the same page, this is a field hearing, an official hearing of the U.S. Congress, The House of Representatives, Energy and Commerce, Subcommittee on Telecommunications and the Internet.

This subcommittee will receive all of the communication issues, including television. Of course, most of our hearings occur in Washington, DC, but sometimes we do try to get out and bring our government back to the people. Because Bobby Rush has such a deep concern for the young people across this country, and in his congressional district, not only did he suggest that we hold a hearing on this topic, but that we also hold it here today. It was his choice of where we held the hearing.

We know that there are many types of these, television, radio, video games, movies, Internet, music. And without a doubt, the media has a tremendous influence on the children of America. We probably all agree that the media has both its upsides and its downsides for children in terms of education and entertainment. And today, we are focusing on the effects on children of one aspect of the media, television, and one aspect of that media, violence.

Television is the most common source of information available to children growing up in our country. Children are not only being entertained, but they're also being educated by TV. Nearly all children, 99 percent, live in a home with a TV. Half have three or more TVs, and over a third have a TV in their bedroom. It is estimated that children today watch 3 to 4 hours of TV every day.

And in light of the growing amount of time children find themselves in front of the TV, the issue of what they're watching becomes increasingly important. Many settings detail the growing incidence of violence on TV, even in children's TV shows.

It has been shown that these scenes of violence do have an impact on children. It is generally accepted that information children receive from these programs cannot help but affect the way that they interact with and view sides. Since 1960, a body of evidence coming from both laboratory research and survey studies has confirmed that there is a causal relationship between the observation of aggression and violence on TV and subsequent aggressive and violent behavior on behalf on the part of the viewer.

And that appears to be especially true for young kids, as much of the research shows that the effect may not just be temporary, but may be sustained over the years. In fact, a number of national committees composed of scholars will review all of the available studies, and come to a similar conclusion, there is a casual relationship between viewing violent TV and subsequent behavior. And when it comes to the impact of TV violence, the number of groups, including the American Psychological Association, The American Medical Association, The U.S. Surgeon General, The National Institute of Mental Health, has confirmed that violence on TV has an influence on aggressive behavior, which it can lead into adulthood.

The three main effects of viewing TV violence include: One, learning aggressive attitudes and behaviors; two, desensitization to pain and to violence; and three, increased fear of being victimized by violence. Interestingly enough, studies have also shown that not all TV violence poses the same degree for harmful effects. There are many ways to portray violence and the consequence of that violence.

For instance, some examples will glorify violence and the perpetrator, others will focus on the negative ramifications of committing a crime. Some experts suggests that not all the portrayals of violence are bad. Some examples can actually have a positive impact on kids. Contectual features, such as the attractive perpetrator, an attractive victim, graphic or extensive violence, rewards and punishments, and humor, can all increase or decrease the risk of harmful effects.

Looking at it another way, do scenes of gunfights in old episodes of Gunsmoke, or Roadrunner pushing Wile E. Coyote off a cliff, has the same effect on kids as grim scenes in "NYPD Blue" or "Law and Order." What about the violent contact of broadcast of the NFL Football, or NHL hockey, or scenes of military firefights in Iraq on the nightly news? How about scenes where the violent actor gets caught by the good guys?

Certainly, TV violence is neither the sole, nor even the most significant cause of restless or violent behavior in kids. But it has been shown to have an effect nonetheless. So, today we want to learn more about those harmful effects, and learn what the parents, educators, and what the communities will do to protect their kids from harmful effects. Ultimately, we will take the information that we learn here back to Washington so that we can see what the government should do, if anything.

In that regard, a number of years ago Congress passed, and I supported the V-Chip Legislation, which paved the way for industry to establish ratings for violence to be incorporated into the TV set so that the parents could know what, if any, content their kids might be exposed to, and to make the decision about what their children could watch accordingly, or even block those shows.

I hope to learn from our witnesses today about their views on this as well. But as we debate the need for any further governmental action, we are compelled to seriously consider the significant limits which the First Amendment of the Constitution imposes on us. We will learn more about that today, too. Because of the significant limits on government action, I suspect it will place an even heavier burden on all of us parents, teachers, religious and community leaders, the TV industry itself to take greater care to address that issue. I look forward to hearing from our witnesses today. And I now recognize that for an opening statement, my friend, great Congressman and good colleague, Mr. Bobby Rush from Illinois.

[The prepared statement of Hon. Fred Upton follows:]

PREPARED STATEMENT OF HON. FRED UPTON, CHAIRMAN, SUBCOMMITTEE ON TELECOMMUNICATIONS AND THE INTERNET

Good morning. Today's hearing is entitled: "The Effect of Television Violence on Children: What Policymakers Need to Know."

I am honored to be here today in my good friend Bobby Rush's congressional district. I am pleased John Shimkus from "down state" is with us today, too.

I want to thank the administrators, faculty—and especially the students—of the Neal F. Simeon Career Academy for hosting us.

Just so we're all on the same page, this is a field hearing of the U.S. House of Representative's Energy and Commerce Subcommittee on Telecommunications and the Internet. This Subcommittee oversees all communications issues, including television. Of course, most of our hearings occur in Washington, D.C., but sometimes we do try to get out and bring our government to the people. And, because Bobby Rush has such deep concern for the young people across this country and in his congressional district, not only did he suggest that we hold a hearing on this topic, but also that we hold it here today.

We know that there are many types of media: television, radio, video games, movies, the Internet, and music. Without a doubt, the media has tremendous influence on the children of America. We'd probably all agree that the media has both its upsides for children in terms of education and entertainment, but it also has its downsides.

Today, we are focusing on the effects on children of one aspect of the media: TELEVISION and one aspect of that medium: VIOLENCE.

Television is the most common source of information available to children growing up in the United States. Children are not only being entertained, but are also being educated by television. Nearly all children (99%) live in a home with a television, half (50%) have three or more televisions, and over one-third (36%) have a television in their bedroom. It is estimated that children today watch three to four hours of television every day. In light of the growing amount of time children find themselves in front of a television, the issue of what they are watching becomes increasingly important.

Many studies have detailed the growing incidence of violence on television, and even in children's television shows. It has been shown that these scenes of violence have an impact on children. It is generally accepted that the information children receive from these programs cannot help but affect the way they interact with and view society. Since 1960, a body of evidence coming from both laboratory research and survey studies has confirmed that there is a causal relationship between the observation of aggression and violence on television and subsequent aggressive and violent behavior on the part of the viewer. This appears to be especially true for young children, as much of the research shows that the effect may not just be temporary, but may be sustained over the years.

In fact, a number of national commissions composed of scholars who have reviewed all of the available studies have come to a similar conclusion—that there is a causal relationship between viewing violent television and subsequent behavior. When it comes to the impact of television violence, a number of groups, including the American Psychological Association, the American Medical Association, the U.S. Surgeon General, and the National Institute of Mental Health, have confirmed that violence on television has an influence on aggressive behavior which can lead into adulthood. The three main effects of viewing televised violence include: (1) learning aggressive attitudes and behaviors, (2) desensitization to violence, and (3) increased fear of being victimized by violence.

Interestingly, studies have also shown that not all television violence poses the same degree of risk for harmful effects. There are many ways to portray violence and the consequences of that violence. For instance, some examples will glorify the violence and the perpetrator; others will focus on the negative ramifications of committing a crime. Some experts suggest that not all portrayals of violence are the same, and some examples can actually have a positive impact on children. Contextual features, such as an attractive perpetrator, an attractive victim, justified violence, extensive or graphic violence, rewards and punishments, and humor, can all increase or decrease the risk of harmful effects.

Looking at it another way, do scenes of gunfights in old episodes of "Gun Smoke" or the "Road Runner" pushing "Wile E. Coyote" off a cliff have the same effect on kids as grim scenes in "NYPD Blue" or "Law and Order"? What about violent contact in broadcasts of NFL football or NHL hockey? Or scenes of military firefights in Iraq on the nightly news? How about scenes where the violent actor gets caught by the good guys?

Certainly television violence is neither the sole, nor even the most significant, cause of aggressive or violent behavior in children, but it has been shown to have an effect nonetheless. So, today, we want to learn more about those harmful effects and learn what parents, educators, and communities can do to protect children from those harmful effects.

Ultimately, we will take this information back to Washington with us as we debate what, if anything, the government can do. In this regard, a number of years ago, Congress passed, and I supported, V-CHIP legislation, which paved the way for industry-established ratings for violence to be incorporated into television sets so that parents could know what, if any, violent content their children might be exposed to and make decisions about what their children watch accordingly, or even block those shows completely. I hope to learn from our witnesses about their views on this as well. But as we debate the need for any further governmental action, we are compelled to seriously consider the significant limits which the First Amendment of the Constitution imposes on us, and we will learn more about that today, too. Because of these significant limits on government action, I suspect it will place an even heavier burden on all of us as parents, teachers, religious and community leaders—and the television industry itself—to take greater care to address this issue.

I look forward to hearing from today's witnesses on this important topic, and I appreciate them being here to help us examine it.

Mr. RUSH. Thank you very much, Mr. Chairman. And, Mr. Chairman, I want to say, first of all, how delighted and gratified that I am that you will come to Simeon High School, to the 4th Congressional District, in hopes to conduct this most important hearing. I want all of us who are present today, all the students to know, that the Chairman didn't have to agree to come here. But he did because he's concerned about this particular issue. He's concerned about what happens to our young people. He's concerned about the effects of violence in America.

Mr. Chairman, I want you to know that, although we come from different political parties, and that what you are doing today shows your character as an individual, as a concerned American, it shows that you have risen above and can rise above partisan differences to make sure that we come together to do those things, and to hear from witnesses, and to really involve ourselves in solving some of the problems that America faces.

And again, Mr. Chairman, I just want to say to you that you are the kind of chairman that will push and pull and make this an issue, a much, much, better Nation. Thank you so much for coming to Simeon High School this morning. I want to thank our inductor, the CEO and the Superintendent of the Chicago Public Schools, and Michael Scott. And I want to thank Dr. Everett for hosting this here at Simeon Academy.

This school is a remarkable school. This school has had its share of violence. I recall so vividly some 20 years ago, the mid-1980's, and the No. 1 college—rather, the No. 1 high school player in the Nation, the basketball player in the Nation was gunned downed not too far from where we're sitting at today. Simeon has risen above those kinds of incidents. But violence is still a part of the day-to-day likely experiences of too many young people, not only here at Simeon, but across this city and across this Nation.

This hearing today is important because it will help us to determine how we can, as Members of Congress, and as members of the telecommunication subcommittee how we can address our responsibility to try to decrease the incidents about violence, particularly as it affects young people today.

Mr. Chairman, you mentioned certain statistics. And I just want you to know that I was alarmed after I looked at some of the studies. The National Television Violence Study indicated that violence was found to be more prevalent in children's program, 69 percent, than any other type of program on TV, which occur at a clip of about 57 percent. The average child who watches 2 hours of cartoons a day may see nearly 10,000 violent incidents a year.

An average city estimated that the averages in pre-school and school-age child, who watch television 2 to 4 hours per day, would have seen 8,000 murders and over a hundred thousand additional acts of violence on television by the time they finished elementary school. These are alarming statistics, Mr. Chairman. We're getting to a point in our society, in fact, we might have already reached that point, where we glorify violence. And these, Mr. Chairman, I believe that we're living in a culture that is violent, so violent, that desensitize our responses, desensitize our activities and desensitize our approach to violence.

And, Mr. Chairman, I want to say to you, again, that I am very glad, grateful, I really believe that this is going to be one of those types of hearings that will be one of our greater achievements of our subcommittee, and our subcommittee has achieved many great achievements over the past years, and I want you to know that this is an important hearing, and thank you so much for being here.

[The prepared statement of Hon. Bobby L. Rush follows:]

PREPARED STATEMENT OF HON. BOBBY L. RUSH, A REPRESENTATIVE IN CONGRESS
FROM THE STATE OF ILLINOIS

Good morning, and welcome to Chicago. I would like to thank Chairman Upton for holding this important hearing in my home city of Chicago. I also would like to thank Arne Duncan, CEO and Superintendent of Chicago Public Schools, Michael Scott, President of the Chicago Board of Education and Principal John Everett for hosting us here today at the exquisite Neal F. Simeon Career Academy a brand new state of the art learning center.

As many of you know, the pervasiveness and effects of television violence continue to be an issue of considerable concern to me. It is well documented that violent programming has an adverse effect on human behavior and attitudes. It encourages violent behavior and influences moral and social values and violence in daily life. However, what concerns me more is the affect that violent programming has on children. There is a strong body of evidence that suggest that exposure to violent acts on television increases aggressive behavior in children in the short-term and long-term.

Study after Study have shown a causal link between violent programming and violent behavior in children. The National television violence study indicated that violence was found to be more prevalent in children=s programming (69%) than in other types of programming (57%). The average child who watches 2 hours of cartoons a day may see nearly 10,000 violent incidents each year. Similarly, a study conducted by researchers from the Annerberg school of communication in Pennsylvania, estimated that the average preschooler and school aged child who watched television two to four hours per day would have seen 8,000 murders, and over 100,000 additional acts of violence on television by the time the child finished elementary school.

As you can see these statistics are alarming. What we have is a society that is not only glorifying violence but it is also becoming desensitized to violence. Gone forever are the days when a parent could simply sit a child in front of the television without adult supervision. Television today requires that responsible parents be proactive in the selection and monitoring of materials that their children are permitted to watch. The issue for us today as policy makers, academia, parents and teachers, is not only how do we shield our children from excessive TV violence but how do we help parents understand and control the programs their children watch.

In 1996, Congress passed legislation as part of the 1996 Telecommunications Act that required television sets to be equipped with an electronic device, called the V-chip, which allowed parents to block certain programming. In addition, Congress encouraged the video and distribution industry to establish an age-based rating system. However, since the advent of the V-chip technology and the age-based ratings system, it was reported by the Kaiser Family Foundation that only half the parents surveyed used the television ratings system to guide their children=s viewing. Also, it was found that only 7% of all parents were using the V-chip technology.

Apparently many parents were not aware that television rating system existed. As for the V-chip many parents who knew about it did not know how to use the technology. It seems that the system Congress has in place is not working. As legislators, we have a responsibility to improve our existing safeguards but also to create better safeguards that will shield our children from inappropriate programming. Currently in Congress, there is pending legislation that would create a safe harbor provision that would restrict excessively violent programming that is harmful to children during the hours when children are likely to be a substantial part of the viewing audience. This "safe harbor" provision is worth examining. That said, I would like to welcome the witnesses and thank them for being with us this morning. Each of you has done considerable work on the issue of TV violence, and I thank you for your time and effort for appearing here today.

Mr. UPTON. Thank you, Mr. Rush. I just want to say, too, as I look at my tenure as chairman, who's been able to do a whole number of issues in bipartisan debates of republicans and democrats working together, I'm very proud of that record. And I recognize now, a good friend also from the State of Illinois, downstate Illinois, and a fellow who really helped lead the charge of getting back his son, which I'm really here to talk about. I never go anyplace without saying something about it. And I would note that I think every member, including you, were a co-sponsor of that, and passed that with honorable, noble men to support this. So, with that, Mr. Shimkus, please give an opening statement.

Mr. SHIMKUS. Thank you, Mr. Chairman. And I also want to thank our panelists, who we'll hear from in a minute, and along with my friend, Bobby Rush, for the warm hospitality. I also want to take time to speak to our guests in the audience there. I taught high school before for years, government history. So, to lay out what's occurring here is, this is an official hearing of your Federal Government on violence on TV. And we're politicians, right here. These are the experts in different fields, and we're going to look to them as they tell us what's right or what's wrong. And maybe give us advice of how we can fix it, or how we can't. How we might not be able to touch it. And hopefully, we take this back, and you see a stenographer over there taking the official recordings, so, then we take the testimony back to Washington. We distill it, and maybe there is a place where, especially if we want to be successful in a bipartisan manner, then get the legislation drafted to try to fix it if it's a possibility. And so, that's what this is. It's not just, you know, coming here, but it's actually the work that we do in Washington, especially in our committee, on a weekly basis. We're just holding a hearing.

Now, Bobby represents the First Congressional District; I represent the 19th District in Illinois. So, we're on the south side of Chicago. My District also goes through Springfield, Illinois, all the way down to Paducah, Kentucky. I represent 30 counties. So, the other important thing to remember is a great diversity that you see from Members of Congress that they're trying to tackle the issues and problems that relate to a national concern. The urban areas and the suburban areas sometimes might have a different approach to rulings, many times they're very simple. And so, it's narrowing those great differences across and dividing them, and hopefully be successful.

I will put in my applaud for putting on my marketing hat, which I've gotten through and will do of one such success. And interestingly more panelist are knowing about it, because that's why I always mentioned it. We have the same concern on what's going on over the TV that we have on the Internet. In fact, the Internet is even a more dangerous place because you can have interaction. And a lot of young men and women get caught up in it, and a lot of harm has been done, especially by adult predators to children. That's why we were able to pass in signing a law a Web site the State prohibits. And I know those people who deal with the Internet say, Well, it helps them. Well, it's not. You can go to www.kids.us, go to the site for kids. There is no hyperlinks, no chat rooms, no instant messaging. It's information-based only, and it is, hopefully—and it hasn't been challenged to the courts yet—suitable for minors under the age of 13.

And my young son, Daniel, who—my 9-year-old and 11-year-old, they're probably too old for this site, even though we made it for kids under 13. My 4-year-old, he'll be 5 in October, is an expert on the kids.us Web site. And there he will go, he will go to Nick Junior, and he'll play the games. And so, he can surf the Web like his big brother. But I can monitor him without the fear that something will pop up that will be very damaging to a 4 or 5-year-old child.

So, that's the part of the success that we have done through hearings, and testimony, and passing legislation. And it is hoped that, as we move forward, that we're able to do that in other venues. And I appreciate the Chairman calling the hearing and, of course, Bobby Rush, and I look forward to the comments from my panelists. And I think that's the one, .kids.us, so we'll see if they go on it.

Mr. UPTON. Well, thank you, Congressman Shimkus. At this point, we're going to hear from our five witnesses. Their statements are made part of the record in their entirety. If you limit your remarks to not more than 5 minutes or so, and summarize what you have to say. You've got a lot of good listeners. And then after that, we're going to follow up with questions. And the three of us will have some questions. But I also understand that last week the students were given an opportunity to write some questions. We're going to let those questions in the written form come up to us, and we'll be able to ask the panelists answers to those questions.

We are joined by Dr. Gary Slutkin, Director of Chicago Project for Violence Prevention, Professor for Epidemiology and International Health, from the UIC Chicago School of Public Health, obviously, here in Chicago. Mr. Jeff McIntyre, Senior Legislative and Federal Affairs Officer, with the American Psychological Association in Washington, DC. Dr. Ronald Davis, Member of the Board of Trustees for the American Medical Association in Washington, DC, Professor Dale Kunkel at Department of Communications from the University of Arizona, Tucson, Arizona. And Professor Rodney Blackman, DePaul College of Law here in Chicago.

Dr. Slutkin, you will start. Make sure that the mics are close so that the students and everybody can be able to hear.

STATEMENTS OF GARY SLUTKIN, DIRECTOR, CHICAGO PROJECT FOR VIOLENCE PREVENTION, PROFESSOR, EPIDEMIOLOGY AND INTERNATIONAL HEALTH, UIC CHICAGO SCHOOL OF PUBLIC HEALTH; JEFF J. McINTYRE, SENIOR LEGISLATIVE AND FEDERAL AFFAIRS OFFICER, PUBLIC POLICY OFFICE, AMERICAN PSYCHOLOGICAL ASSOCIATION; RONALD M. DAVIS, MEMBER, BOARD OF TRUSTEES, AMERICAN MEDICAL ASSOCIATION; DALE KUNKEL, PROFESSOR, DEPARTMENT OF COMMUNICATION, UNIVERSITY OF ARIZONA; AND RODNEY JAY BLACKMAN, DePAUL COLLEGE OF LAW

Mr. SLUTKIN. Chairman Upton, Congressman Rush, Congressman Shimkus, thank you very much for this opportunity to speak with you today. I'm Gary Slutkin, I'm a physician trained in internal medicine and infectious disease control. I worked for a health organization for 10 years in its behavioral of epidemics.

I now run the Chicago Project for Violence Prevention, which is a multi-prong setting interventions to reduce shootings in Chicago and other Illinois neighborhoods. We have a 45 to 65 percent drop in shootings using this new technology for reducing violence. I wanted to quickly go to three items for the evidence, what we can do about it, and then a little bit about the larger picture.

The evidence to television and other video violence affect children and adolescent behavior is, in my opinion, unequivocal and certain. It is serious and dangerous matter, and not trivial. The industry may argue that not every study shows these effects to their kids. Well, almost every study does, and the best reviews of studies done by George Comstalker (phonetic), totally unbiased senior, one of the most senior epidemiologist in, frankly, the world, has come to the same conclusions.

Both short-term and long-term effects that's been stated repeatedly, why does a case, as obvious for our chairman to mention the kind of effects, I'll review them briefly, but why is this the case? It's absolutely obvious, the extraordinary regularity, the magnitude and intensity of the violence make it appear as if it's normal. Imitation and modeling are of many ways that face these in young children and adolescence learned. That's how they select behaviors. We use this very well in advertising. That is, again, why the cigarette industry wanted to have cigarette smoking on the television regularly, and that's why it was removed.

And, in fact, as you might imagine for very young children, and perhaps even others who are watching, may differentiate very, very little from things that are commercials, to things that are television, as you blockview, just sit there and let images come in. The way to promote anything, any behavior, whether it's immunizing your children, using Gatorade, drinking Coke, or violence, is to show it over and over and over and over, as if it were normal. This is the way to do it. If someone else, for example, from another country or from another society were to be seeing this on types of our programming, and into our homes, I would probably find a way to do something about it.

What to do about it? This is more up to you than up to us. I realize that the media is principally driven by commercial return. Now, since the media is driven by commercial return, the use of violence, sex and graphically changing images, those are things that grab the eye and the brain, and make it up stiff like Velcro. And so, it's very hard to look away when violence is happening, sex is happening, or when images change fast. So, that's the technology that they use to hold your eye to the screen, so that you'll be there for the commercial effects. And this is the principle reason why it's done.

I think that regulation is desirable, I think a completely unregulated society that is driven purely by commercial return has got to turn into an unhealthy society. I mean, we have to put our values into somewhere. And I'm sure there is going to be a lot of discussion on this. I would like to add an additional suggestion that I learned from work at World Health, that it's also possible.

I remember being there myself, personally or professionally involved in the bashing of an industry. And I won't do that now. But principally, it's for professional and technical reasons, as well as I'm not going to speak against. And I've learned that it's possible to change behavior by positive new programming on a small level. And for just by way of example, in Europe where there is somewhere in the tens of thousands of daily episodes on subjects slightly sexual, acts that are either shown or implied without a condom, by getting a certain amount of condom promotion shown to a certain level, is uptake to 70 percent condom used was achieved through European countries. So, that it's possible to overcome some of this because people will begin to evaluate the others in the context. But this has to be done in a professional way with credible knowledge and alternative shown.

The last thing I want to spend a minute on is just talk about the larger context. The U.S. Has the highest homicide rate of all developed countries in the world. In fact, it's not higher by a small amount, it's higher by five to twenty times more. So, we have a global reputation that independent of international behavior, but surely on the basis of our domestic behavior, our homicide rates are high. We're known as a very aggressive and violent society statistically and in other ways.

The media took a part of this. But there also needs to be a national strategy to reach this. I've worked on national and global strategy, and we don't have one. I mean, we do not have one. Having more police and having more afterschool programs, are not all that's needed. I mean, there has to be specific outreach programs, community disapproval programs, and things that show results, programs to a sufficient scale, and we're trying to do. And anything other than increasingly more dangerous society that we're living in. Thank you.

[The prepared statement of Gary Slutkin follows:

PREPARED STATEMENT OF GARY SLUTKIN, DIRECTOR, THE CHICAGO PROJECT FOR VIOLENCE PREVENTION

EFFECTS OF TELEVISION AND MEDIA VIOLENCE ON CHILDREN

I am Gary Slutkin. I am a physician trained in internal medicine, and infectious diseases. I worked for the World Health Organization for 7 years and was responsible for reversing epidemics such as tuberculosis, cholera, and AIDS, and have special training in designing interventions and reversing behavioral epidemics. I supported the Uganda AIDS control program—the only country in Africa to have reversed its AIDS epidemic and I now run the Chicago Project for Violence Prevention and CeaseFire Illinois which is reliably obtaining 45-65% reductions in shootings in some of the highest risk communities in the country.

I would like to talk about three things—the evidence that television and media play a role in affecting children, what we can do about it, and thirdly, look at the larger picture of what we will need to do to substantially reduce the violence in our society.

1. The evidence

The evidence that television and other media violence affect child and adolescent behavior is now *unequivocal, and certain.* Violence, in particular repeated violent events on television and in the movies, increases the likelihood of children engaging in violent acts themselves. This is serious and dangerous and not a trivial matter. The industry can argue that not every study shows this; in fact almost every study does.

Media images of violence especially the extraordinary regularity of it, makes it appear as if this is normal behavior. Babies and young children look for models, and what to imitate for social approval; the media provide some of this "guidance" for their behavior. This is not a small matter—this is the usual way of learning—and what we see others do is more powerful than what we are told to do and told not to do. We—people—are driven by what we think other people do—and what we think will "get" us something—from money to prestige to other forms of attention or approval.

Behaviors are driven by social expectations—i.e. "norms," this means by what you think other people do. This is true for all behaviors. This is one of the reasons we began to limit cigarette smoking on television—this was considered important—and I agree—because of the bad effects in particular for the health of children.

We show or promote what *behaviors "we"* want to be performed—immunizing children, buying gym shoes, drinking Coke, eating a cereal, bringing children for immunization, using seat belts, using designated drivers, smoking or not smoking, or performing violence. Whatever you promote will be taken up, and in some proportion to the amount or intensity of promotion. Advertisers know this and public health professionals know this—whether it is for good or bad, or for this or that—whatever is promoted will be taken up to some degree. We are that susceptible. And the mind, and especially the young mind, does not easily sort between programming, real life and even commercials.

The literature on the effects of violence on television on children is more compelling than most people think. There is a near unanimity of scientific opinion on the effects. And further, besides encouraging violent behaviors themselves, and resulting in more aggression following watching violent programs, other important negative mental health consequences are also being seen in the research now. These effects—which have also been well demonstrated—include children having more anxiety, more fear, more isolation, and desensitization to violence—which causes children to care less and help others less. This has been shown in playground experiments.

It would be hard to better design something to promote violent behavior and to interfere more with our values and with how our society functions, than to consciously "*program*" violence over and over again beaming into our homes each night from an electric screen onto our minds. *If persons outside of our own citizens, for example another government, were projecting these images to us, we would find a way to stop it immediately.*

2. What to do about it.

The feasibility of constraining this programming is probably limited by the success of commercial return. We know that the television viewing system is designed to compete for your eye and mind through "visual stickiness" to the viewing screen, so that your eyes and other senses then remain available during the paid advertising slots, which are similarly designed to keep you present. You can check this yourself—as you are stuck as if by Velcro in the time period, while these images are inserted into your brain. Three things keep your eyes fixed most intently (and thereby your brain fixed). Eye—brain research shows that your are best kept "focused" *involuntarily*—for reasons that are instinctive, by images of violence or sex, and by rapidly changing images/screens (which in "real life" might be scenes of danger). The media are using this knowledge to manipulate our attention, and thereby arguably unfairly taking advantage of what keeps us stuck. This is why violence is used in programming.

Regulation is desirable. I realize that we are not today in a climate of increasing regulation. I realize that further regulation of many harmful events may be less feasible today as our society is even more permissive of these effects, despite actual and known dangers, since there is a desire to not interfere with commercial activity. However it is probably worthwhile to consider why this violent programming is so prevalent, and more tolerated than other matters, for example consensual sex. Is there regulation of showing sex on television? How was this distinction drawn? What is more harmful consensual sex or murder? Which should be considered more normal and acceptable? How does murder compare with smoking cigarettes?

A direction of even further loss of government regulation will have serious consequences for our society. A society that is motivated without sufficient attention to research despite capital gain, and without more guidance or regulation may be heading for even further disastrous consequences.

3. Other possible solutions

I am not the one to say whether regulation in this area is legal or politically practical, despite commercial gains by the industries that advertise competitively using violence as a tactic, to keep our attention. But we do need to be awake to this.

I would like to bring forward one other parallel track that we should very seriously pursue if we share the objectives of maintaining free speech under any and all conditions, despite consequences that we know are present, but still trying to reduce violence and the acceptability of violence in our society. Programming which promotes alternatives to violence and shows the unacceptability of violence if programmed at the 5% level from credible role models could off-weigh a substantial part of the effects if performed in a specific and pre-designed way. It is beyond the scope of this testimony to describe this, but success in other fields has been performed from similar approaches. I am not talking about "shows about non-violence," but a specific type of social marketing toward deglamorizing and discrediting violence with endpoints that would be agreed upon by the industry and by government. I would be happy to discuss this with interested persons.

4. The larger context—homicide and violence in America

Last, I want to spend just a minute to put this in a larger context. The U.S. has the highest homicide rate of all rich countries. In fact this rate is not just larger but substantially larger (5-20 times), and is not due to guns alone. This is a global anomaly that is remediable. It is clear that the media violence is drastically excessive and should not really be acceptable in particular for children, but we must recognize that we as a society, country, and nation have a particular problem. This is both within our borders and otherwise. We must develop a strategy for dealing with this. There is at this moment no strategy for dealing with this that would be considered an actual strategy, and even 100,000 more cops would not be a "strategy," but just one piece of what is needed. This view is accepted even by Chief Bratton, previously of New York City and now of Los Angeles. More is needed than police.

The community piece of violence reduction and the intervention component are now scientifically grounded and there are now opportunities for developing a much more specific and reliable set of methods that should reduce urban and other homicides by 40—70%. This would result in reduced crime, reduced costs of crimes, better use of state budgets than for prisons, release of funds for education spending, and urban renewal and economic development for many urban and rural communities. It is urgent for public health and community benefit that the country develop a specific outcome based, scientifically grounded, and already community demonstrated approach to reducing violence, and take this to scale for the benefits of dozens or hundreds of communities.

At a minimum, we need to immediately develop in our most violent cities, active outreach, public education, high-risk alternatives, and community involvement strategies that are specific, measurable and show results. Even after the more cops on the street programs, rates of violence still remain enormously higher than should be the case in our society. CeaseFire type programs as are now being applied in Chicago and other sites throughout the country, and are urgently needed in more cities. A National CeaseFire Partnership is in the early stages of development. For the younger children, I think specifically designed social marketing approaches could also add substantially.

I am very grateful for this opportunity to speak with you about all of our concerns about the violent nature of our society today, the rapidity in which we as individuals and groups move into this predictable pattern, and how we are continuing to teach this to our children. Unless we fully accept the trend that is in process, and take the specific actionable steps—with or without regulation of the media—we will be living in an even much dangerous world.

References

Comstock, G. 1991. *Television in America.* Newbury Park, CA: Sage Publications.

Donnerstein, Edward and Linz, Daniel. 1995. "The Mass Media: A Role in Injury Causation and Prevention." *Adolescent Medicine: State of the Art Reviews* vol. 6, no.2:271-284. Philadelphia, PA: Hanley & Belfus, Inc.

Hornik, Robert C. 2002. *Public health communication: evidence for behavior change*. Mahwah, NJ: Lawrence Erlbaum Associates, Inc.

Huston, A.C., Donnerstein, E., Fairchild, H., Feshbach, N.D., Katz, P.A., Murray, J.P. Rubin-stein, E.A., Wilcox, B. and Zukerman, D. 1992. *Big World, Small Screen: The Role of Television in American Society*. Lincoln, NE: University of Nebraska Press.

Liebert, R.M. and Sprefkin. 1998. *The Early Window: Effects of Television on Children and Youth*. New York: Pergamon.

Murray, J.P. and Salamon, G. 1984. *The Future of Children's Television: Results of the Markle Foundation/Boys Town Conference*. Boys Town, NE. The Boys Town Center.

National Institutes of Mental Health. 1982. *Television and Behavior: Ten Years of Scientific Progress and Implications for the Eighties* vol. 1. Rockville, MD: U.S. Department of Health and Human Services.

Mr. UPTON. Thank you very much.

Mr. McIntyre.

STATEMENT OF JEFF J. McINTYRE

Mr. McINTYRE. Good morning, Mr. Chairman, members of the House Energy and Commerce Subcommittee on Telecommunications and the Internet. I am Jeff McIntyre, and I'm honored to be here in Chicago to represent the American Psychological Association.

I've conducted years of work related to children and the media as a negotiator for the development of a television rating system. As an advisor to the Federal Communications Commission's V-Chip Task Force, as a member of an informal White House Task Force on navigating the news media, as a member of the steering committee for the Decade of Behavior Conference on Digital Childhood, and most importantly, as a representative of the research concerns of the over 150,000 members/affiliates of the American Psychological Association. I also have an appointment on the Oversight Monitoring Board for the current television rating system.

At the heart of the issue of children and the media is a matter long addressed by psychological research. The effects of repeated exposure of children to violence. The media violence issue made its official debut on Capitol Hill in 1952 with the first of a series of congressional hearings. That particular hearing was held in the House of Representatives before the Commerce Committee. The following year, 1953, the first major Senate hearings was held before the Senate Subcommittee on Juvenile Delinquency, who convened a panel to inquire into the impact of television violence on juvenile delinquency.

There have been many hearings since the 1950's, but there has only been limited change until recently. Media violence reduction is fraught with legal complications. Nevertheless, our knowledge base has improved over time with the publication of significant and landmark reviews. Based on these research findings, several concerns emerge when violent material is aggressively marketed to children.

Foremost, the conclusions drawn on the basis of over 30 years of research contributed by American Psychological Association members, including the Surgeon General's report in 1972, National Institute of Mental Health's Report in 1982, and the industry-funded 3-year National Television Violence Study in the 1990's, show that the repeated exposure to violence in the mass media places children at risk for: Increases in aggression; desensitization to acts of violence, and unrealistic increases in fear of becoming a victim of violence, which results in the development of other negative characteristics, such as mistrust of others, et cetera.

Now, if this sounds familiar, it is because it is the foundation upon which representatives of the public health community comprise of the APA, the American Academy of Pediatrics, and the American Medical Association issued a joint consensus statement in the year 2000 on what we absolutely know to be true regarding children's exposure to violence in the media. Certain psychological facts remain and are well established in this debate. As APA member Dr. Rowell Huesmann stated before the Senate Commerce Committee, just as every cigarette you smoke increases the chances that some day you will get cancer, every exposure to violence increases the chances that some day a child will behave more violently than they otherwise would.

Hundreds of studies have confirmed that exposing their children to a steady diet of violence in the media made our children more violence prone. The psychological processes here are not mysterious. Children learn by observing others. Mass media and the advertising world provide a very attractive window for these observations.

The excellent children's programming such as Sesame Street, and prosocial marketing such as that around bicycle helmets that exists, is to be commended and supported. Psychological research shows that if what is responsible for the effectiveness of good children's programming and prosocial marketing is that children learn from their media environment. And if children can learn positive behaviors via this medium, they can learn negative ones as well.

The role of rating systems in this discussion merits attention. There continues to be concern over the ambiguity and the implementation of the current television rating system. It appears that rating systems are undermined by the marketing efforts of the very groups responsible for their implementation and effectiveness. That, Mr. Chairman, and members of the subcommittee, displays a significant lack of accountability and has to be considered when proposals for industry self-regulations are discussed.

Also undermined here are parents and American families. As the industry has shown a lack of accountability in the implementation of the existing rating system, parents have struggled to manage their family's media diet against misleading and contradictory information. For instance, marketing an R-rated film to children who are under 17. While the industry has made some information regarding the ratings available, more information regarding content needs to be made more accessible more often. Just as with the nutritional information, the content labeling should be available on the product and not hidden in a distant Web site or in the occasional pamphlet.

Generally speaking, most adults see advertising as a relatively harmless annoyance. However, advertising directed at children, especially in young children that features violence, generates concern. The average child is exposed to approximately 20,000 commercerials per year And that's only for television. It doesn't include print or the Internet. And much of this is during weekend morn or weekday afternoon programming. Most of the concern stems not from the sheer number of commercial appeals, but from the inability of some children to appreciate and defend against the persuasive intent of marketing. Especially advertising featuring violent product.

A recent Federal Trade Commission report on the marketing of violence to children heightens these concerns. As a result of the Children's On-Line Privacy Protection Act, the Federal Trade Commission has ruled that parents have a right to protect their children's privacy from the unwanted solicitation of their children's personal information. We would argue that, based on the years of psychological research on violence prevention and clinical practice in violence intervention, parents also have the right to protect their children from material that puts them at risk of harm. With the considerations that are in place for children's privacy, the precedent for concern about children's health is well established.

Decades of psychological research bear witness to the potential harmful effects on our children and our Nation if these practices are continued. Chairman Upton and subcommittee members, thank you for your time, and please regard the American Psychological Association as a resource to the committee as you consider this and other issues.

[The prepared statement of Jeff J. McIntyre follows:]

PREPARED STATEMENT OF JEFF J. MCINTYRE ON BEHALF OF THE AMERICAN PSYCHOLOGICAL ASSOCIATION

Good morning, Mr. Chairman and Members of the House Energy and Commerce Subcommittee on Telecommunications and the Internet. I am Jeff McIntyre and am honored to be here in Chicago to represent the American Psychological Association.

I have conducted years of work related to children and the media as a negotiator for the development of a television ratings system, as an advisor to the Federal Communications Commission's V-Chip Task Force, as a member of an informal White House Task Force on Navigating the New Media, as a member of the steering committee for the Decade of Behavior Conference on Digital Childhood, and most importantly, as a representative of the research and concerns of the over 150,000 members and affiliates of the American Psychological Association. I also have an appointment on the Oversight Monitoring Board for the current television ratings system.

At the heart of the issue of children and the media is a matter long addressed by psychological research—the effects of repeated exposure of children to violence. The media violence issue made its official debut on Capitol Hill in 1952 with the first of a series of congressional hearings. That particular hearing was held in the House of Representatives before the Commerce Committee. The following year, in 1953, the first major Senate hearing was held before the Senate Subcommittee on Juvenile Delinquency, who convened a panel to inquire into the impact of television violence on juvenile delinquency.

There have been many hearings since the 1950's, but there has been only limited change—until recently. Media violence reduction is fraught with legal complications. Nevertheless, our knowledge base has improved over time, with the publication of significant and landmark reviews. Based on these research findings, several concerns emerge when violent material is aggressively marketed to children.

Foremost, the conclusions drawn on the basis of over 30 years of research contributed by American Psychological Association member—including the Surgeon General's report in 1972, the National Institute of Mental Health's report in 1982, and the industry funded, three-year National Television Violence Study in the 1990's—show that the repeated exposure to violence in the mass media places children at risk for:

• increases in aggression;
• desensitization to acts of violence;
• and unrealistic increases in fear of becoming a victim of violence, which results in the development of other negative characteristics, such as mistrust of others.

16

If this sounds familiar, it is because this is the foundation upon which representatives of the public health community—comprised of the American Psychological Association, the American Academy of Pediatrics, and the American Medical Association issued a joint consensus statement in 2000 on what we absolutely know to be true regarding children's exposure to violence in the media.

Certain psychological facts remain are well established in this debate. As APA member Dr. Rowell Huesmann stated before the Senate Commerce Committee, just as every cigarette you smoke increases the chances that someday you will get cancer, every exposure to violence increases the chances that, some day, a child will behave more violently than they otherwise would.

Hundreds of studies have confirmed that exposing our children to a steady diet of violence in the media makes our children more violence prone. The psychological processes here are not mysterious. Children learn by observing others. Mass media and the advertising world provide a very attractive window for these observations.

The excellent children's programming (such as Sesame Street) and pro-social marketing (such as that around bicycle helmets) that exists is to be commended and supported. Psychological research shows that what is responsible for the effectiveness of good children's programming and pro-social marketing is that children learn from their media environment. If kids can learn positive behaviors via this medium, they can learn the harmful ones as well.

The role of ratings systems in this discussion merits attention. There continues to be concern over the ambiguity and implementation of current ratings systems. It appears that ratings systems are undermined by the marketing efforts of the very groups responsible for their implementation and effectiveness. That, Chairman Upton and members of the Subcommittee, displays a significant lack of accountability and should be considered when proposals for industry self-regulation are discussed.

Also undermined here are parents and American families. As the industry has shown a lack of accountability in the implementation of the existing ratings system, parents have struggled to manage their family's media diet against misleading and contradictory information. (For instance, marketing an R rated film to children under 17.) While the industry has made some information regarding the ratings available, more information regarding content needs to be made more accessible, more often. As with nutritional information, the content labeling should be available on the product and not hidden in distant websites or in the occasional pamphlet.

Generally speaking, most adults see advertising as a relatively harmless annoyance. However, advertising directed at children, especially at young children, that features violence generates concern. The average child is exposed to approximately 20,000 commercials per year. This is only for television and does not include print or the Internet. Much of this is during weekend morning or weekday afternoon programming. Most of the concern stems not from the sheer number of commercial appeals but from the inability of some children to appreciate and defend against the persuasive intent of marketing, especially advertising featuring violent product.

A recent Federal Trade Commission report on the Marketing of Violence to Children heightens these concerns. As a result of the "Children's On-Line Privacy Protection Act" the Federal Trade Commission has ruled that parents have a right to protect their children's privacy from the unwanted solicitation of their children's personal information. We would argue that, based on the years of psychological research on violence prevention and clinical practice in violence intervention, parents also have the right to protect their children from material that puts them at risk of harm. With the considerations in place for children's privacy, the precedent for concern about children's health and safety is well established.

Decades of psychological research bear witness to the potential harmful effects on our children and our nation if these practices continue. Chairman Upton and Subcommittee members, thank you for your time. Please regard the American Psychological Association as a resource to the committee as you consider this and other issues.

Mr. UPTON. We certainly have in the past. Thank you very much. Dr. Davis.

STATEMENT OF RONALD M. DAVIS

Mr. DAVIS. Chairman Upton and members of the subcommittee. My name is Ronald Davis, I'm a preventive medicine physician practicing in Detroit, and residing in East Lansing, and I'm a member of the Board of Trustees of the American Medical Association.

On behalf of the AMA, I am pleased to be here today to discuss the effects of television violence on children.

As one that was born in Chicago, and who attended medical school just a few miles from where we are today, at the University of Chicago, I'm particularly pleased to be in this city and in this wonderful school for this hearing this morning. I speak to you not only as a physician, but also as a father of three sons. And like most parents in the United States, my wife and I have had a hard time patrolling around the violent entertainment that comes into our own household.

As we all know, television has a huge presence in most children's lives. Almost every home in America has a television, and most homes have more than one. Studies show that kids, on average, watch television 3½ hours a day. One in five kids watches more than 35 hours of TV each week. Our children today are constantly bombarded with violence in TV shows, movies, video computer games and music. Media violence has increased and is more and more graphic. The AMA has been concerned for years about violence on TV and its impact on the physical and mental health of children and teens.

The AMA first expressed concern about the public health impact of violent television in the early 1950's. Since then the AMA has adopted strong policy opposing TV violence. Our policy also recognizes that TV violence is a risk factor and threatens children's health and welfare.

In July, 2000, as mentioned by Jeff McIntyre, the AMA joined with the American Academy of Pediatrics, American Psychological Association, and other prominent groups. In particular, a joint statement of Entertainment, Violence, and Children. A copy of that statement is attached to our written testimony. The joint statement recognizes that TV programs can be an important educational tool for children. But it points out that the lessons learned from violence in TV programs and other entertainment media can be very destructive.

Research for more than one thousand studies indicates that watching entertainment violence can increase aggressive values, attitudes, and behavior. The effect on children is complex and vary. And some kids are affected more than others. But it is clear that children who seek a lot of violence are more likely to think that violence is acceptable and is the way to settle conflicts. And younger children are always the most affected. Viewing violence may lead to real life crimes.

TV violence by itself, as has been mentioned, is not the only factor that leads to youth aggression, anti-social attitudes and actual violence. There are other causes, such as family breakdown, peer pressure and easy access of guns and other weapons. But there is no question that TV violence has negative effects on children and adds to the level of violence in our society. Violence is a public health threat, and we need to confront all of its causes.

What is the physician's role in all of this? First, physicians should educate themselves about the harmful effects of TV violence on children. Second, as educators, physicians should talk to their patients, the children themselves, if old enough, or their parents about television. They need to ask how much TV is watched and the type of programs. As physicians we need to counsel our patients that watching violent TV shows can be bad for the children. The parents need to monitor and control their children's exposure to violence through TV and other entertainment media.

Physicians should consider the role of media when treating patients. For example, with children who are hyperactive or aggressive, or who complain of nightmares or other sleep problems, physicians should ask about their TV viewing habits. Limiting rotation to the types of programs the patient watches may be part of a recommended treatment plan Finally, as advocates, physicians should be involved in community and school activities, if possible, just like we're doing here today. They can speak to parents or school groups, or directly to children about the impact of TV violence. They should also speak out for more responsible TV programs.

Chairman Upton, all of us have important roles to play in curving the harmful exposure of our children to accepted violence on TV and in other entertainment media. The AMA and our physicians look forward to working with you and the subcommittee and others to implement strategies to make that happen.

[The prepared statement of Ronald M. Davis follows:]

PREPARED STATEMENT OF RONALD M. DAVIS, MEMBER, AMERICAN MEDICAL ASSOCIATION BOARD OF TRUSTEES

Good morning Chairman Upton, and Subcommittee members. My name is Ronald M. Davis, MD, and I am a member of the Board of Trustees of the American Medical Association (AMA). I am a preventive medicine physician and serve as Director of the Center for Health Promotion and Disease Prevention at the Henry Ford Health System in Detroit, Michigan. I am pleased to be able to testify today on behalf of the AMA. The AMA commends the Subcommittee for holding today's hearing on television violence and its effects on children.

Television and other forms of visual media play an enormous role in everyday life, particularly in the lives of children and adolescents. While television serves in the education and socialization of children, there are also a number of health problems associated with the excessive watching of television—independent of content—such as the rising rates of childhood obesity. In addition, an extensive body of research documents a strong correlation between children's exposure to media violence and a number of behavioral and psychological problems, primarily increased aggressive behavior. The evidence further shows that these problems are caused by the exposure itself.

Physicians, particularly those who treat children, are only too aware of the pervasive effects of television, movies, music videos, and computer and video games on modern life and the concern felt by many over the violent content of these media. There is an established body of evidence documenting the troubling behavioral effects of repeated exposure to media violence. For the past several decades, the physician and medical student members of the AMA have been increasingly concerned that exposure to violence in media is a significant risk to the physical and mental health of children and adolescents. America's young people are being exposed to ever-increasing levels of media violence, and such violence has become increasingly graphic.

Today 99% of homes in America have a television. American children, ages 2-17, watch television on average almost 25 hours per week or 3½ hours a day, with almost one in five watching more than 35 hours of TV each week. Twenty percent of 2 to 7-year-olds, 46% of 8 to 10-year-olds, and 56% of 13 to 17-year-olds have TVs in their bedrooms, a practice which the AMA urges parents to avoid. Studies have shown that 28% of children's television shows contain four or more acts of violence, and that before he or she reaches the age of 18, the average child will witness more than 200,000 acts of violence on television, including 16,000 murders. One survey revealed that of the shows that contained violence, three quarters of them demonstrated acts of violence that went unpunished.

Violence in all forms has become a major medical and public health epidemic in this country. The AMA strongly abhors, and has actively condemned and worked to reduce, violence in our society, including violence portrayed in entertainment media.

The AMA has long been concerned about the prevalent depiction of violent behavior on television and in movies, especially in terms of its "role-modeling" capacity to potentially promote "real-world" violence. We have actively investigated and analyzed the negative effects that the portrayal of such violence has on children, and for almost 30 years, have issued strong policy statements against such depictions of violence.

Concerns about the public health impact of violent television emerged relatively soon after its development as an entertainment media. In 1952, the AMA first expressed its concerns over the potential impact of violent television programming on children in an editorial in the *Journal of the American Medical Association.* At its 1976 annual meeting, the AMA adopted a policy supporting research on the impact of media violence. A resolution was also adopted at the same meeting that declared the AMA's "recognition of the fact that TV violence is a risk factor threatening the health and welfare of young Americans, indeed our future society." In 1982, the AMA reaffirmed "its vigorous opposition to television violence and its support for efforts designed to increase the awareness of physicians and patients that television violence is a risk factor threatening the health of young people." This policy remains in force, and has been expanded to include violence in entertainment media other than television, such as movies, videos, computer games, music and print outlets.

Since the AMA first raised the issue in 1952, a compelling body of scientific research has confirmed that our original concerns were well-founded. Over 1000 studies, including reports from the Office of the Surgeon General, the National Institute of Mental Health, and the National Academy of Sciences, as well as research conducted by leading figures in medical and public health organizations, point overwhelmingly to a causal relationship between media violence and aggressive behavior in some children. The research overwhelmingly concludes that viewing "entertainment" violence can lead to increases in aggressive attitudes, values and behavior, particularly in children. Moreover, exposure to violent programming is associated with lower levels of pro-social behavior.

The effect of "entertainment" violence on children is complex and variable, and some children will be affected more than others. But while duration, intensity and extent of the impact may vary, there are several measurable negative effects of children's exposure to such violence:

- Children who see a lot of violence are more likely to view violence as an effective way of settling conflicts and assume that acts of violence are acceptable behavior.
- Viewing violence can lead to emotional desensitization towards violence in real life. It can decrease the likelihood that one will take action on behalf of a victim when violence occurs.
- Entertainment violence feeds a perception that the world is a violent and mean place. Viewing violence increases fear of becoming a victim of violence, with a resultant increase in self-protective behaviors and a mistrust of others.
- Viewing violence may lead to real life violence. Children exposed to violent programming at a young age have a higher tendency for violent and aggressive behavior later in life than children who are not so exposed. Longitudinal studies tracking viewing habits and behavior patterns of a single individual found that 8-year old boys, who viewed the most violent programs growing up, were the most likely to engage in aggressive and delinquent behavior by age 18 and serious criminal behavior by age 30.

In July 2000, at a Congressional Public Health Summit, the AMA joined the American Academy of Pediatrics, the American Academy of Child and Adolescent Psychiatry, the American Academy of Family Physicians, the American Psychiatric Association and the American Psychological Association in issuing a "Joint Statement on the Impact of Entertainment Violence on Children." The Joint Statement acknowledges that television, movies, music and interactive games are powerful learning tools and that these media can, and often are, used to instruct, encourage and even inspire. The Joint Statement, however, also points out that when these entertainment media showcase violence, particularly in a context which glamorizes or trivializes it, the lessons learned can be destructive. A copy of this joint statement is attached to our testimony.

Entertainment violence is certainly not the sole, or even necessarily the most significant, factor contributing to youth aggression, anti-social attitudes and violence. Family breakdown, peer influences, the availability of weapons, and numerous other factors may all contribute to these problems. However, there is no question that entertainment violence does have pathological effects on children, and the AMA believes that because violence is a public health threat, careful consideration must be given to the content of entertainment media. As part of its strategy to reduce violence, the AMA has supported past efforts by network broadcasters in adopting advance parental advisories prior to airing programs that are unfit for children, strong and effective television and movie ratings systems, "V" Chips that can screen out violent programming, and most recently, DVD-filtering devices.

We are not advocating restrictions on creative activity. In a free society, there must be a balance between individual rights of expression and societal responsibility. We do believe, however, that the entertainment industry must assume its share of responsibility for contributing to the epidemic of violence in our society, and should exercise greater responsibility in its programming content.

Physicians have important roles to play in reducing children's involvement with violent media by serving as educators, advisors and advocates. All physicians need to recognize that violence in America is a major public health crisis, and that media violence contributes to this crisis. Physicians need to educate themselves about the harmful effects on children of viewing or listening to violence in entertainment media, and discuss these effects with parents and children old enough to understand such information. Patients can then make more informed choices about the amount and type of television they watch. Patients will better understand the need for parental involvement in decisions about movie, music, video, computer and video game content and the impact of various forms of media on eating habits, physical activity, and family life in general. Physicians should serve as role models by using television sets in office and clinic waiting rooms for educational purposes only and having media literacy materials available.

As clinicians, physicians have the opportunity to consider the role of media as part of a broader biopsychosocial evaluation when evaluating specific presenting problems. For example, in children being evaluated for aggressive, oppositional or hyperactive behaviors or for nightmares or other sleep complaints, inquiring about the child's violent media-related activities may identify a contributing factor that could be modified as part of a treatment plan.

As advocates, many physicians are involved in community activities that seek to reduce the public's over-utilization of media and/or the amount of violent and other problematic content in media materials. This may include such things as speaking about this topic at medical meetings, to parent or school groups, or directly to children; joining local "media watch," "media literacy," or other groups; or participating in national organizations, such as the AMA, that promote these goals.

The AMA will continue to speak out about violence in the media, especially its role in contributing to the overall level of violence in our society. We will continue to urge the media industry to reduce the amount of violence in television programming, movies, music, video games and the Internet; depict successful nonviolent solutions for anger and conflict; and depict accurately the pain, remorse, and other consequences of violence and violent behavior on individuals, families and society.

We appreciate the opportunity to share our views on a matter of such importance to the health of Americans.

———

[Below is a document signed in July by the American Academy of Pediatrics (AAP) and five other prominent medical groups about the connection between media and violent or aggressive behavior in some children. Please also access the AAP Media Matters page.]

JOINT STATEMENT ON THE IMPACT OF ENTERTAINMENT VIOLENCE ON CHILDREN
CONGRESSIONAL PUBLIC HEALTH SUMMIT

July 26, 2000

We, the undersigned, represent the public health community. As with any community, there exists a diversity of viewpoints—but with many matters, there is also consensus. Although a wide variety of viewpoints on the import and impact of entertainment violence on children may exist outside the public health community, within it, there is a strong consensus on many of the effects on children's health, well-being and development.

Television, movies, music, and interactive games are powerful learning tools, and highly influential media. The average American child spends as much as 28 hours a week watching television, and typically at least an hour a day playing video games or surfing the Internet. Several more hours each week are spent watching movies and videos, and listening to music. These media can, and often are, used to instruct, encourage, and even inspire. But when these entertainment media showcase violence—and particularly in a context which glamorizes or trivializes it—the lessons learned can be destructive.

There are some in the entertainment industry who maintain that 1) violent programming is harmless because no studies exist that prove a connection between violent entertainment and aggressive behavior in children, and 2) young people know that television, movies, and video games are simply fantasy. Unfortunately, they are wrong on both counts.

At this time, well over 1000 studies—including reports from the Surgeon General's office, the National Institute of Mental Health, and numerous studies conducted by leading figures within our medical and public health organizations—our own members—point overwhelmingly to a causal connection between media violence and aggressive behavior in some children. The conclusion of the public health community, based on over 30 years of research, is that viewing entertainment violence can lead to increases in aggressive attitudes, values and behavior, particularly in children.

Its effects are measurable and long-lasting. Moreover, prolonged viewing of media violence can lead to emotional desensitization toward violence in real life.

The effect of entertainment violence on children is complex and variable. Some children will be affected more than others. But while duration, intensity, and extent of the impact may vary, there are several measurable negative effects of children's exposure to violent entertainment. These effects take several forms.

- Children who see a lot of violence are more likely to view violence as an effective way of settling conflicts. Children exposed to violence are more likely to assume that acts of violence are acceptable behavior.
- Viewing violence can lead to emotional desensitization towards violence in real life. It can decrease the likelihood that one will take action on behalf of a victim when violence occurs.
- Entertainment violence feeds a perception that the world is a violent and mean place. Viewing violence increases fear of becoming a victim of violence, with a resultant increase in self-protective behaviors and a mistrust of others.
- Viewing violence may lead to real life violence. Children exposed to violent programming at a young age have a higher tendency for violent and aggressive behavior later in life than children who are not so exposed.

Although less research has been done on the impact of violent interactive entertainment (video games and other interactive media) on young people, preliminary studies indicate that the negative impact may be significantly more severe than that wrought by television, movies, or music. More study is needed in this area, and we urge that resources and attention be directed to this field.

We in no way mean to imply that entertainment violence is the sole, or even necessarily the most important factor contributing to youth aggression, anti-social attitudes, and violence. Family breakdown, peer influences, the availability of weapons, and numerous other factors may all contribute to these problems. Nor are we advocating restrictions on creative activity. The purpose of this document is descriptive, not prescriptive: we seek to lay out a clear picture of the pathological effects of entertainment violence. But we do hope that by articulating and releasing the consensus of the public health community, we may encourage greater public and parental awareness of the harms of violent entertainment, and encourage a more honest dialogue about what can be done to enhance the health and well-being of America's children.

DONALD E. COOK, MD, *President, American Academy of Pediatrics;* CLARICE KESTENBAUM, MD, *President, American Academy of Child & Adolescent Psychiatry;* L. MICHAEL HONAKER, PHD., *Deputy Chief Executive Officer, American Psychological Association;* E. RATCLIFFE ANDERSON, JR. MD, *Executive Vice President, American Medical Association;* AMERICAN ACADEMY OF FAMILY PHYSICIANS; and the AMERICAN PSYCHIATRIC ASSOCIATION

Mr. UPTON. Professor Kunkel.

STATEMENT OF DALE KUNKEL

Mr. KUNKEL. Thank you very much for the opportunity to testify today. I've studied children and media issues for over 20 years, and am one of the senior researchers who led the National Television Violence Study in the 1990's, a project widely recognized as one of the largest scientific studies of media violence. In my remarks here today, I will briefly report the key findings in that project, as well as summarize the state of knowledge in the scientific community about the effects of media violence.

I was impressed with all the opening statements from members this morning, and particularly yours, Mr. Chairman. You echoed one of the lines that I often present, and that is to list the major organizations of public health agencies that are already drawn a conclusion that you're hearing from the panel here today. The Surgeon General, The National Academy of Science and so on. We might add to that list that the broadcasting industry, the BMAE, the National Cable Television Association, your friend, Jack Lempke, who heads the MPAA, all of these individuals and organizations have also acknowledged that media violence contributes to real world violence and aggression.

And I encourage the committee to hold them accountable for those statements and for behavior that is consistent with that knowledge. Because we heard so much about some of the summaries, I'm going to skip some of my remarks and only include in the record the documents that research reviews, and turn directly to a research that I've been involved with the National Television Violence session. Much of that work emphasized the importance in examining differences in the ways in which violence is presented on television and the implications that those differences hold from the effects that result from viewing violent material.

Simply put, not all violence is the same in determining the potential for harmful effects on child viewers. The nature of the context that surrounds the violence matters, and that is important. For example, consider a violent act that has the following feature. It is committed by a repugnant character who no one would wish to imitate. It clearly depicts part of the sufferings by victims, and it results in strong negative consequences for the perpetrator of the violence. That kind of portrayal would actually minimize the risk of the most harmful effects for viewers, because it does not glamorize nor sanitize the depiction of violence.

In contrast, consider a very different type of violent portrayal. One that is committed by an attractive or popular character, who is a potential role model for children, that depicts unrealistically mild harm to the victim who is attacked. And that conveys power and status for the perpetrator or attracts the approval of others in the program. This type of portrayal, by glamorizing and sanitizing the depiction of violent behavior, has a much stronger risk of leading to harmful outcomes in the viewer.

Research conducted by myself and colleagues at four universities as part of the National Television Violence Study documents a very unfortunate trend in the context surrounding most violent depictions on the television. Our final report, which was based on the analysis of roughly 10,000 programs across three television seasons, concluded that the manner in which violence is presented on television follows the latter example that I just traced. That is to say, that the most pattern associated with violent portrayal on TV involved contextual features such as: Not showing a realistic degree of harm for the victim; not showing the pain and suffering that's realistically associated with violent attacks; and not showing the serious long-term negative consequences of violence.

These patterns were present in the large majority of violent portrayals across all channels and at all times of the day. In contrast, programs that included a strong anti-violence theme accounted for less than 4 percent of all shows containing violent content.

Now, these data are troubling, but they're not new. They serve to underscore that the way in which most violence is depicted on television does, indeed, pose a serious risk of harm for children. Whether or not violence on television might be reduced in quantity, it could certainly be presented in more responsible action, thereby diminishing the risk of harm to child viewers. This is one potential avenue for addressing concerns in this area that, in my view, has not been actively explored.

In sum, the research evidence clearly establishes that the level of violence for TV is a substantial cause for concern. Content analysis demonstrates the violence of a potential aspect of TV programming that enjoys remarkable consistency and stability over time. And effect research, including correlational, experimental, and longitudinal design, all converge to document the risk of harmful psychological effects on child viewers is very potent.

Collectively, these findings from the scientific community make clear that television violence is a troubling problem. I applaud this subcommittee for considering the topic and exploring potential policy options that may reduce or otherwise ameliorate the harmful effects of children's exposure to television violence.

[The prepared statement of Dale Kunkel follows:]

PREPARED STATEMENT OF DALE KUNKEL, DEPARTMENT OF COMMUNICATION, UNIVERSITY OF ARIZONA

Thank you for the opportunity to testify today before the Subcommittee.

I have studied children and media issues for over 20 years, and am one of several researchers who led the National Television Violence Study (NTVS) in the 1990s, a project widely recognized as the largest scientific study of media violence. In my remarks here today, I will briefly report some key findings from the NTVS project, as well as summarize the state of knowledge in the scientific community about the effects of media violence on children.

Media Violence: The Importance of Context

Concern on the part of the public and Congress about the harmful influence of media violence on children dates back to the 1950s and 1960s. The legitimacy of that concern is corroborated by extensive scientific research that has accumulated since that time. Indeed, in reviewing the totality of empirical evidence regarding the impact of media violence, the conclusion that exposure to violent portrayals poses a risk of harmful effects on children has been reached by the U.S. Surgeon General, the National Institutes of Mental Health, the National Academy of Sciences, the American Medical Association, the American Psychological Association, the American Academy of Pediatrics, and a host of other scientific and public health agencies and organizations.

In sum, it is well established by a compelling body of scientific evidence that television violence poses a risk of harmful effects for child-viewers. These effects include: (1) children's learning of aggressive attitudes and behaviors; (2) desensitization, or an increased callousness towards victims of violence; and (3) increased or exaggerated fear of being victimized by violence. While exposure to media violence is not necessarily the most potent factor contributing to real world violence and aggression in the United States today, it is certainly the most pervasive. Millions of children spend an average of 20 or more hours per week watching television, and this cumulative exposure to violent images can shape young minds in unhealthy ways.

Much of my research has emphasized the importance of examining differences in the ways in which violence is presented on television, and the implications such differences hold for the effects that result from viewing violent material. *Simply put, not all violence is the same in terms of its risk of harmful effects on child-viewers.* The nature and context of the portrayal matters. For example, consider a violent act that has the following features:

—it is committed by a repugnant character who no one would wish to emulate;

—it clearly depicts the harms suffered by victims;

—and it results in strong negative consequences for the perpetrator.

This type of portrayal would actually minimize the risk of most harmful effects for viewers, because it does not glamorize or sanitize its depiction of violence. In contrast, consider a different type of violent portrayal;

—one that is committed by an attractive or popular character who is a potential role model for children;

—that depicts unrealistically mild harm to the victim who is attacked,

—and that conveys power and status for the perpetrator or attracts the approval of others in the program.

This type of portrayal, by glamorizing and sanitizing the depiction of violent behavior, has a much stronger risk of leading to harmful outcomes in the viewer.

Research conducted by myself and colleagues at four universities as part of the *National Television Violence Study* documents an unfortunate trend in the context surrounding most violent depictions on TV. Our final report, which was based on the analysis of approximately 10,000 programs across three television seasons, concluded that the manner in which most violence is presented on television actually enhances rather than diminishes its risk of harmful effects on child-viewers. That is, the most common pattern associated with violent portrayals on TV involved contextual features such as:

—*not showing* a realistic degree of harm for victims;

—*not showing* the pain and suffering realistically associated with violence attacks;

—and *not showing* the serious long-term negative consequences of violence.

These patterns were present in the large majority of violent portrayals across all channels, and at all times of day. In contrast, programs that included a strong anti-violence theme accounted for less than 4% of all shows containing violent content.

Implications of the Findings

These data are troubling, though they are not new. They serve to underscore that the way in which most violence is depicted on television poses a serious risk of harm for children. It does not *have* to be that way. Independent of whether or not violence on television might be reduced in quantity, it could certainly be presented in more responsible fashion, thereby diminishing its risk to child viewers. This is one potential avenue for addressing the concern about media violence that, in my view, has not yet been adequately explored.

In sum, the research evidence in this area establishes clearly that the level of violence on television poses substantial cause for concern. Content analysis studies demonstrate that violence is a central aspect of television programming that enjoys remarkable consistency and stability over time. And effects research, including correlational, experimental, and longitudinal designs, converge to document the risk of harmful psychological effects on child-viewers. Collectively, these findings from the scientific community make clear that television violence is a troubling problem for our society. I applaud this Subcommittee for considering the topic, and exploring potential policy options that may reduce or otherwise ameliorate the harmful effects of children's exposure to television violence.

Mr. UPTON. Thank you.

Professor Blackman.

STATEMENT OF RODNEY JAY BLACKMAN

Mr. BLACKMAN. I would like to express my pleasure for being here. And I teach constitutional law and First Amendment issues, and I taught these subjects for many years. The question of violence can be examined in the context of various forms of anti-social communication and how the court deals with it. The explicit sexual graphic, sexual material in its (inaudible) and expressions of violence. At one time, the court allowed plaintiffs to recover for what was called a group libel expression of hatred directed at a particular group.

In more recent years the Supreme Court has refused to allow— or seemed to refuse to allow recovery for new libel or hate scenes directed at a group. The lesson constitutes rare and specific individuals, or I want to say it constitutes the defamatory material directed at specific individuals. With respect, it is sexually explicit material. The court has limited sex issue, sexually explicit material to that which is regarded as it seems that which is happening appeals to the parameter of this and lacks artistic—literary, artistic, scientific valu taken as a whole. Pornography that is out of scene is allowed in the media.

The question of what would be the key question toward violence has not been resolved. But it looks as though the Supreme Court would be very remarkable to allow me for contacting—researching the prohibition expression to violence with one exception with the broadcast media where the broadcast suggest a monopoly sense of the broadcast band return it connects with the broadcaster that the broadcast majority rules the pieces and the statements.

George Carl gave a talk in which he use several of the verdicts that are not ordinarily used in the broadcast media. And the Supreme Court held a sanction of the broadcaster, the broadcaster center on two o'clock in the afternoon. Violence that promotes anti-social act, killing or suicide in adolescences, has not been found to justify a tort of action against the broadcaster. Because the causal relationship between the broadcast of the anti-social message and the act is not sufficiently close. A group of women have attempted to get—sustain an ordinance that prohibited violence against women. And the courts have held that unless the material comes within the definition of obscenity, fewer (inaudible) has offensive likely to look at the political—I'm sorry—literally artistic liberal sector governing, taken as a whole, it could not be prohibited.

So, the road of those who would engage in content-base restrictions on violence is for others to seek one. That does not mean, however, that all reforms and activity on the part of those who wish to restrict violence in school.

John Stewart, a proponent of listing fair government action involving self-regarding harmful acts is not only the kind of thing that he believes, namely, a worthy opponent to the harmful violence. And I believe that the depiction of violence can be harmful. The idea of promoting V-Chips that are requiring salespeople to inform customers of how to use a V-Chip. That, too, will be possible. Go into Hollywood and see the producer and directors produce violence that will technically lead to the kids, that, too, would be harmful. So, would not all of us would run (inaudible) analysis. Thank you.

[The prepared statement of Rodney Jay Blackman follows:]

PREPARED STATEMENT OF RODNEY JAY BLACKMAN, PROFESSOR, DEPAUL COLLEGE OF LAW

I would like to express my opposition to any broad based governmental restriction of media and internet violence. I would like to do so for several reasons.

First, I will admit that depictions of violence on TV, the movies or on the internet, available to children, particularly repeated depictions, increases the likelihood of children engaging in acts of violence. But I am still opposed to any broad based censorship of the media and the internet to protect children.

One reason is that it gives the impression of government acting as Big Brother. It was Joseph Stalin who claimed to be the engineer of human souls. To a minor degree and in a seemingly benign way, broad based censorship of media and internet violence available to children lends itself to this approach. The assumption underlying this approach is that the government should mold what images children receive in order to create a more socially adjusted child. While having social well adjusted children is a laudable goal, any broad based censorship in one area has the potential for encouraging other restrictions (the slippery slope argument). Are depictions of violence that children can see any more justified than depictions of sex or hatred? Once government starts down this road in one area, any logical limit to governmental regulation in other areas is weakened. The sum of such regulations, though not each individual one taken separately, could move our citizenry, and not just the young, toward a substantially restricted ability to see images and express thoughts.

A second reason is that, over the long run, it may restrict our liberty without being effective. The underlying assumption is that it is only external stimulus that causes people, children and adults, to act in an anti-social way. If we could only eliminate the external stimulus, we would solve the problem of anti-social behavior. But this view seems simple minded. Ted Bundy said that his violent acts against women were triggered by looking at violent pornography. This cannot be the whole story. The vast majority of men could look at depictions of violent acts against women and would likely become disgusted or bored and stop looking. While the external stimulus might be the immediate cause in specific instances, something in the human brain of some people is also going on. Could anyone seriously argue, for example, that the neo-Nazi, Matthew Hale, developed his views because of some Nazi film that he saw? Under the view that I am espousing some people (mostly boys and men) have either been poorly raised by their parents or parent substitutes or else have some genetic flaw that makes them particularly violent. If this is so, then censoring the images that children (or adults) receive in the media or internet would have little or no long term effect on such people.

A third reason is that any broad based restriction is likely to be ineffective because it restricts what children and adults can see more completely than the public would tolerate. If children cannot see violent cartoons on TV, then they might gravitate to violent cartoon comics. If children and adults, cannot see or read violent material more generally, they will gravitate even more to violence in sports—boxing, wrestling, football, hockey even baseball and basketball. In order to protect children fully, the government would have to regulate what appears on news broadcasts. No images of people shooting people in Iraq would be allowed. Then too, the *Bible* and *Koran* contain depictions of violence. Should these be barred as well?

A fourth reason is that efforts to protect children through broad based restrictions of violence on TV or the internet are likely to run afoul of the Supreme Court's understanding of the First Amendment. While the Court has allowed government to restrict depictions of obscene material (pornography that appeals to the prurient interest, is patently offensive and lacks serious literary, artistic, political or scientific value) and sexual depictions of children (whether obscene or not), it has so far not allowed for media restrictions of violence. The one case I am aware of in this area was a city's effort to prohibit degrading or violent depictions of women. Since the ordinance was not limited to the narrow obscenity exception to First Amendment protected speech, the federal courts struck it down. The Court has also struck down statutes that restrict what adults can see even though they have been enacted ostensibly to protect children. As the Court puts it, adults cannot be limited to what is fit for children. Thus, if the net result of a broad based restriction so as to limit what adults can see on TV or in the movies, I believe it would run afoul of similar Court pronouncements. As to the Internet, the Court has not yet determined whether it would accept a restriction on what children can access based on community standards when the result would enable the most restrictive community to determine what children could access in the most permissive communities.

What I would call a narrowly based statute, one that, for example, requires that salesmen selling TVs explain to buyers how to use the V-Chip (assuming the TV has one), a labeling statute as to what is unfit for children, or a statute that prohibits depictions of violence in cartoon shows in the morning hours, probably would be upheld by the Court and would not unduly restrict our First Amendment liberties.

Mr. UPTON. Well, thank you very much.

What we're going to do at this point, I think that each of us here on the panel, members of the panel, usually ask a question, and then we go to the question the students have submitted. I'm going to play Devil's advocate here for a moment. I'm a dad, I've got two kids. I've got a high school junior and I've got a seventh grader. And as parents, my wife and I are always very concerned about what they do, what shows they watch, computer, and all of that, and we're nice people, we're very good parents. And I know that parental influences is a major, major element.

And I concur with the studies that have been done. My wife and I are so concerned about the access that our kids have in making sure that they are properly handling what they're seeing. In fact, today's USA Today newspaper, I don't know if any of you saw it, and I would say off the top, I'm 51 years old, it's still hard for me to say that, and I have watched TV shows, from my viewing as a teen, it's a great escalation in terms of violence and for our kids. And all those specific scenes, we're exposed to the specifics and have a lot more violence than their parent's kids see on TV at all the different hours, et cetera.

Things are much more violent today than they were, 20, 30 years ago. But yet, the USA Today, today's story, list the crime rates in the paper. It said that the crime rates have a steady low last year. And looks at crime statistics go back into the early 1990's. A comparable number in 1993, the violent crime rate was 50 per a thousand people. In 2003, there was, it says here, that "amounts have grown from a violent crime rate of an assault, intentional assault, armed robbery", it stood at 22.6 victims for every thousand, age 12 and up to about double. It was double in 1993 than it is today.

So, we see a real climb in crime rates. Yet, at the same time, we see, at least in my view, the amount of increase in the kind of violence. If they are exposed to it, and all people are exposed. I just— and all people are exposed, I just welcome the democratic to be here, and to advise: Why do you get that, those numbers are the way that they are? Dr. Slutkin.

Mr. SLUTKIN. The overall crime rate is unlikely to limit the amount on television as it is. Because as it's been pointed out, there is other influences, too. I would like——

Mr. UPTON. Grand Auto Theft wasn't a game that is on the videos.

Mr. SLUTKIN. I would like to point out, though that these rates, that albeit somewhere between a fourth and a half down from what they were at their highest peak, are still 25 times higher than they are in other countries. And it's a situation that is substantially different than that in other developed countries. So, we have a completely out of control situation that is not only out of control, you know, it is like having the police not doing anything, and then suddenly they're doing some pieces of their job. But the community aspect of this, the parental aspect of this, the advertising and promotion of the violence, all that stuff is still in there. So, I think that some interventions have been put into place. But there is no complacency of where the rates are now.

Mr. UPTON. It does make a point, by the way, that there are more people in jail than ever before.

Mr. SLUTKIN. And as you've pointed out, so, what have we got there? We have a society in which we're promoting violence, regularizing violence, and catching those who do it, and putting them in jail. So, it's obviously not a correct situation.

Mr. UPTON. Anybody else have a comment?

Mr. KUNKEL. Yes, please. Mr. Chairman, when you talk about crime rates and so forth, it's important to underscore that no one is suggesting that media violence is the sole or even the primary contributor to real world violence and aggression. We are asserting it is a significant contributor. Let's draw a little comparison here. If you wanted to reduce heart attacks in this country, how would you do that? Well, you would look at what are the risk factors that contribute to heart attacks. And those that include cigarette smoking is one risk factor. If you're over a certain weight, then you're obese, and that's a risk factor. If you have high stress in your job, that's a risk factor. There can be a history of heart disease in your family, that's a risk factor.

Now, from the medical perspective, the way you're going to reduce heart attacks is to diminish those risk factors. If you took away one risk factor in the United States, there was never—no smoking was allowed in this country, we're going to increase it and say if no one smoked, then would you still have heart attacks? Absolutely, you still would.

Now, let's look at the situation with the crime rate and so forth. Your suggestion is that there is more violence, or there is certainly more graphic violence in the media today. But the data that we have from content studies, if you look over the last 4 years, actually show that the violence in the media and in the television is very consistent and stable. In fact, that's one of the most interesting points, remarkably stable. And if you look at the big picture, yes, I think crime rate and violence in the real word is down, but I believe that that is because the progress in the country is engaged in a large number of initiatives and efforts to reduce violence. But I don't think that you can use that as an argument to say that real world violence isn't affected by the violence that we see. Research is far too compelling in the other direction.

Mr. BLACKMAN. I would like to get out of the area and talk more generally. There are a number of reasons why there are more crimes in the United States than there are in other countries. One is the fact that we have a society that people are different. And when you're—everybody that has crime rates have the same background, you might think that they are related to you. Go back a few hundred years and you might be less prone to engage in violence if you're around it. It's a very disciplinary action. We don't have that in this country. We also have a very mobile society where people with relatively polished backgrounds can move up. We, in our society where there are jobs available, we have a society where, at least to some extent, there are drugs available, there is alcohol available. And we have a society with a high rate of breakdown in family life. And all of those factors contribute to the amount of violence.

How much is the—the thought of the violence in the main aspect of the human mind to create the young adolescent, and—and teenage, and young adults they (inaudible). I remember reading an article that I had, pages of the New York Times, by a novelist, Michael Shovone, some months ago, when he said that children have violent thoughts. They will be independent of the amount of media about violence, true the media market increases the likelihood of violence. But it's a multi-dimensional problem I suspect in focusing only on this one aspect which has a potential for limiting what adults can watch. It may not be the appropriate approach.

Mr. UPTON. Thank you. And a quick comment, and then Mr. Rush has some questions.

Mr. DAVIS. Chairman Upton, I just wanted to make a point that violence in the media may have other effects besides those criminal activities. I think we heard about research linking violence in the media and aggressive behavior or abusive behavior. We've seen statistics showing an increase only in activity, for example, through the years, and this is something that the AMA has been speaking out on in recent years. The published studies in the Journal of the American Medical Association on voting, and pointing out how for too long we've taken that problem for granted. And we need to take it seriously and have a zero tolerance approach to bully activity in the schools, and in other places where youth congregate, because of its serious aspects on our children.

Mr. UPTON. Mr. Rush.

Mr. RUSH. Thank you, Mr. Chairman. Mr. Chairman, first of all, I'd like to take a moment to thank all of you panelists for coming from across the Nation here for this hearing. And I also want to thank my colleague, Mr. Shimkus, for his presence here also.

I want to concur with some of you. That's a compliment. Mr. Chairman, 4 years ago I lost my son from a violent act. And the thing that really I focus on determines the type of violences that are occurring almost on a daily basis. In some of our homes, in our streets, is that we are desensitized to something that we see, and the television portrayals of violence. We don't see the effects of after that. One of the things that really It just hit me so hard, that that kind of pain and tragedy, the kind of gut-wrenching reaction to violence for my family, not only for those convicted, but also for the perpetrators of violence, and the kind of trauma, the ongoing trauma that occurs, that never gets portrayed; the mothers in pain. The pride of the mothers get portrayed. So, the kind of textual aspects of a violent act, and the result of the violent act, never gets away. But I believe that you pick your own in terms of the contextual responsibility that we have here.

I want to just tell the students here some of the questions that you had per your remarks. And I'm going to start with just trying to answer some questions. But I would like to ask the panelist, Mr. McIntyre, if you will comment on the parent's responsibilities. Where does the parental responsibilities come in as we discuss TV viewership which portrays violence? What is my responsibility as a parent?

Mr. MCINTYRE. I would say that they start day one, and perhaps even a little before day one, to start thinking about how to prepare healthy viewing habits for your kids. The thing that can be tricky for parents in this is two points. One is that, you know, everybody is different, all individuals are different. And so all kids are different, too. And so the parent really needs to be in touch with where their own child or children are so that they can kind of monitor and help with the healthy media habits around the kids. What strengths, their weaknesses or virtues that they want their child to develop. If the child is showing some instances of pleading, or increased fear, of being a victim, then they're going to want to be aware of the violence that they're looking at over in the media. Part of the good thing about the ratings that we have now, is that parents can tweak their preferences based on whatever decisions they make about their kid, if they are concerned about violence, if they're concerned about sexual behavior, then it's up to the parents to honor those paths. But the parents do need to have reliable information to be able to do that. We do think that the television industry can do a little in providing more accurate and more reliable information. But ultimately, it's the parents that we're trying to empower this.

Mr. KUNKEL. Would you indulge in another response, Mr. Chairman?

Mr. RUSH. Sure.

Mr. KUNKEL. I think that everyone concurs that parents have a significant role, primary role to play in protecting their children from TV violence. You have got to look at the data, however, to appreciate that many parents are not sensitized to this topic. Indeed, there is a substantial proportion of homes in America that there is always constantly a television on in homes. And what that we need to keep in mind is that a household where the television set is basically left on all day whether anyone is watching it or not. Television is on during meals and so forth. And whatever programming is coming along the channel that it's on, is allowed to play regardless of its activity in the content. Those are numbers that represents millions of homes in this country. So, if you believe all the data that you've heard today, if you believe that media violence has contributed to real world violence and aggression, then while it's important to look for parents to play a role here, parents can't be the only solution.

If there are representatives from the television industry here today, they would advocate that it's the parent's responsibility, not their responsibility. And that the parents have to do their job, and we have a big problem here. And I don't think that realistically because we are up against a multi-billion dollar industry that now permeates our culture such that to engage in your immediate consumption. You cannot like media violence. And I think one of the real shames is, that just as you point out that we are desensitized, we don't respond to see violence in the media on television.

In fact, when you read stories of a murder or a crime, unless we know the victim, we don't respond with the pain and grief and anguish that we should, because we read those stories too often. The only time we respond with great sensitivity is when the numbers of people killed are so high that they grab our attention because they have what, a new record. And it's a shame that things have come to that point. We need to be more sensitive to media violence, and this dramatic part that we need to give parents the tools and the training to help them do their job to sensitize their children.

Mr. RUSH. Mr. Chairman, I just want to see something just for a moment. I really want to ask the audience, just by the raising of hands, how many students here in this auditorium in the last year know someone, either a relative, or a friend, or a friend of a friend, knows someone who has been killed by violence in the last year? Would you raise your hands?

[Students raise hands.]

Mr. RUSH. Okay. Thank you. How many students here in the last year know someone or is either a friend, or knows someone who knows someone, or a family member who has had a violent act, who has been injured by a violent act in the last year?

[Students raise hands.]

Mr. RUSH. Thank you very much. I ask that because this is, indeed, a problem that we are constantly experiencing. I know in my experiences that between the hours of 12 and 2 o'clock—well, let's say 10 and 2 p.m., every Saturday, most young—a lot of young—significantly young to what I prefer, of someone who has been killed, are attending funerals. It's probably one of the major gathering places for someone who has been killed. On Saturday it's a place for young people to gather between 10 a.m. and 2 p.m. Thank you.

Mr. UPTON. Mr. Shimkus.

Mr. SHIMKUS. Thank you, Mr. Chairman. And I want to thank my colleague, Bobby Rush here, for doing that. I was going to ask the question, too. But I think his question really highlights the challenges that we have in the national level on different areas. If you ask that in my high school in my district, I don't think you would get a hand. You wouldn't get a hand raised. Now, we would have kids who are drinking and driving, who have other activities of violent crimes. So, I thank you for asking that. Let me follow along with the panelists, like you did last, and I'll look around, of the students here, poke your friends next to you because I want to get hands up on this. How many of you all have a TV in your household, one TV?

[Students raise hands.]

Mr. SHIMKUS. How many, one or more, one or more?

[Students raise hands.]

Mr. SHIMKUS. Okay. How many have three TVs in your home?

[Students raise hands.]

Mr. SHIMKUS. How many of you have this is a question the chairman let me ask before. How many have a TV in your bedroom?

[Students raise hands.]

Mr. SHIMKUS. How many of you watch more than 3 hours of TV a day?

[Students raise hands.]

Mr. SHIMKUS. More than 2 hours a day?

[Students raise hands.]

Mr. SHIMKUS. Okay. I'm not done. How many know or understand that there is a TV rating system out there?

[Students raise hands.]

Mr. SHIMKUS. Can anyone explain it to me?

Mr. RUSH. Just one person.

Mr. SHIMKUS. Can anyone explain the rating system to me, anyone out there? Yes, right there in the white. Stand up, I can't hear you. Speak from the upper diaphragm.

UNIDENTIFIED SPEAKER. Well, on TV it will tell you what it's rated, like, PG, or PG-13, or rated R.

Mr. RUSH. What does it mean?

UNIDENTIFIED SPEAKER. Uh?

Mr. RUSH. What does it mean?

UNIDENTIFIED SPEAKER. PG-13 is for little kids, rated R is for big kids.

Mr. SHIMKUS. All right. How many of you know anything about what they call a V-Chip? Has any of you ever had problems watching something you wanted to watch because your parents turned it on, or used it? How many never heard of V-Chip, raise your hands.

[Students raise hands.]

Mr. SHIMKUS. This is good for us. I mean, we read, we do surveys, we can hear testimony. But really, we have audiences that are here from Washington, DC. We don't usually ask these questions. But the difference is, they are tailored to students and are being paid to sit in and listen to what you all have just listened to. Or there are visitors, and they can leave at any time they want, and they just listen for a few minutes, and they get bored, and they usually walk out.

Although, there are some public interests that are concerned about what we're going to do. So, this is really—you are experiencing what happens in Washington on a hearing. And I appreciate your asking questions. The last thing I would say is for the folks who need AMA, and anyone else concerned, there is legislation this year ongoing, which is another major problem in our schools, probably we're not successful into moving in this year, but we call "teeing it up" for the realization of next year, and if you're interested in involving with that as it pertains to this issue, we would really encourage your participation. And, Mr. Chairman, thank you.

Mr. UPTON. Thank you. Well, Congressman Rush has with him a list of questions that the students have prepared. And it is at this point we'll take the next 15 or 20 minutes, if there is that many questions. And, Bobby, we will let you read the questions and get a response, and at which point, then we'll conclude.

Mr. RUSH. Thank you, Mr. Chairman. Just to take a note that these questions, and there are some outstanding questions, I want to congratulate the students here at Simeon High School for very insightful questions. Question No. 1, and any of the panelists, if you will, if you can respond to this: "Do you feel the government has a right to regulate what is shown on television?"

Mr. UPTON. Just do a yes or no answer.

Mr. SLUTKIN. Yes, I think they have some responsibility.

Mr. McINTYRE. Yes, they have some responsibility.

Mr. DAVIS. I would say, yes, in terms of rating systems and possibly controlling the content of child programs.

Mr. KUNKEL. Are there limits to what the government can do? Yes. But can the government convene and rate some regulations in this area? Yes.

Mr. BLACKMAN. I would agree that the time regulation might be feasible. And I would be opposed to comment other than that. But a rating system might also be too small.

Mr. RUSH. The next question is: "What are your ideas of what parents should do to limit their children from watching violence on television?" How can parents limit their children from watching violence on television? And I guess maybe we can talk a little more about the V-Chip and what the V-Chip does.

Mr. SHIMKUS. Take them out of the bedrooms.

Mr. UPTON. Let's start over here.

Mr. RUSH. This time let's start over here. Professor Blackman, what ideas do you have for what parents should do to limit their children from watching violence on television?

Mr. BLACKMAN. My understanding is that there is a significant set of parents that don't know how to use the V-Chip. They have brought TV fairly recently into the V-Chip and this is going to be there. So, perhaps through the schools educating parents who have televisions on how to use the V-Chip would be a helpful concern. And also requiring that televisions sold with the V-Chip, that the salesperson is trained to explain how to use them.

Mr. KUNKEL. I'll be brief. But I'd like to make two points. And the first is that most television viewing is not planned. That is to say, the most common way to view television is to go to the set when you have available time, turn it on, and on the channels that they show us. The odds are better than 50/50, you're going to encounter a violent program. So, what a parent can best do is to plan their children's viewing with the child. That is to say, you open up the TV Guide every week; you find the programs that are going to be valuable; you either adjust your schedule and watch it that time, and take advantage of new technology, like the digital video records, so you can capture that program, and watch it at your convenience. If you were going to take a trip to the library, you wouldn't walk into the library aimlessly, go up a particular aisle and pull a book off at random. It's not how we read. Why is that the way we watch television? So, that would be one point.

My second point here is, that in the context of a discussion about the V-Chip, the V-Chip is an important tool for parents. But it may not be the tool for the age range that we're meeting with here today. Young people at this age are going to be, I think, negotiating with their parents what's appropriate to view, and being in agreements with the context with the parents, assuming the parents is proactive in keeping that responsibility.

The V-Chip is really designed more for the younger child audience, when the parent can't always be at the TV set, but is nearby in the home. And so, it's an aid, I think, primarily to younger children rather than the older group.

Mr. RUSH. Dr. Davis.

Mr. DAVIS. I would say that the parents, first of all, need to know what their kids are watching. And I won't be popular with the kids in the audience here in saying this, but having televisions in the bedrooms, as a parent of three sons, I don't think is a great idea, because you don't know what they're watching. I think total time in front of the television, or playing video games, or playing computer games, needs to be controlled by their parents. Having a television on during meals is something we always avoid in our own household. Because that's the time where parents and their children connect and find out about their day, talk about issues that might be prominent.

And I think parents need to set limits on the kind of shows that kids are allowed to watch. As has been mentioned, it's hard to find any program that doesn't have some violence in it. But some programs have expensive and gratuitous violence that runs throughout the program, and those are the kinds of programs that parents need to have their children avoid watching.

Mr. MCINTYRE. I'm going to step in and say, you know, I think the biggest thing the parents can do is to know their kids. That so many times parents get distracted by jobs and bills and whatnot. And they're not familiar with what's going on in their kids' lives. And if they get their kids look the way I see, the parents think that there is something to talk about in the kitchen or in the refrigerator. You know, you got to know what your kids are about. You don't know your kids. You think that, you know, for one child, you know, the parents may approve of them watching Jackie Chan or Jet Li, or those sort of movies. But for another kid, I think that represents significant risks, and the parents are too distracted by the things going on in their world, and don't have tons of patience with their kids in the media, and that's what we address.

Mr. SLUTKIN. Yeah, I think the planning and the limiting of time and knowing are such a—I just would like to add one particular thing. And not every parent will be there or agree, but I think it might be useful that you have a conversation about what television is. And for those of us who watch a little bit of television, to ask ourselves, are we just squawking down and being lazy and letting ourselves be in the situation we're in. The television is stronger than you are. In other words, the television is larger than your mind. Whether than you being larger than it, and being able to control it, so you can be able to turn it off, which you become a little stronger.

Mr. UPTON. I have a quick question for the audience again. And that is: Well, there are three ways you can get TV, one is satellite, one is cable, the other one is over the air. So, I'd like to know where they are. How many people have watched their TV through cable? Raise your hands.

[Students raise hands.]

Mr. UPTON. Okay. And how many people watch through satellite?

[Students raise hands.]

Mr. UPTON. All right. And is there anyone here that has just over-the-air, just an antenna?

[Students raise hands.]

Mr. UPTON. All right. Thank you. Next question.

Mr. RUSH. Mr. Chairman, I think most of the questions are, again, are the same type. Well, let me ask this, and this is a good one here. It says, "Violence is part of everyday life, not just on television." If violence is taken off the TV because of children, what will the government, or what should the government do to retain— not retain—to reduce violence in our community on a daily basis with for our children?

Mr. MCINTYRE. There is a large array of programs that we can discuss, and discuss the merits and values of—that can address the problems as much as individuals vary, communities vary, and those that seek violence and individual communities have to be approached as well. Everything from educational programs to prenatal health, to the presence of guns.

One of the concerns that we have at the APA is a qualitative increase in violence. Not necessarily that the numbers are going up, but we're saying that violence isn't about getting out back in the schoolyard, punching each other, giving each other a black eye. But it's about, you know, whipping out a nine millimeter and settling it that way. That, there is a wide variety of.

Mr. DAVIS. As a physician, I'd like to mention a couple examples of what we in the medical profession can do. One is for physicians to look for signs of violence when their patients come in with problems. For example, physicians need to be attuned to domestic violence when a woman comes in with trauma. And then we put out guidelines for what other physicians need to be doing to look for that kind of thing.

What they also mention is a program we had in LaPorte Hospital in Detroit, we've seen some horrible statistics on kids coming into the emergency room with trauma. Initially, they might be a victim of an assault, and then a year later they might be back with a stab wound, and then a year after that with a gunshot wound. And our statistics show that a few percentage that we were discovering were dead in 5 years. So, we said to ourselves, why not intervene with these kids the first time we can, or they go down that inevitable cascade of worse and worse trauma and violence.

And so, we had a program in LaPorte Hospital where we connect kids after they presented a trauma, we call it, The Teen of Enrichment Program. And we bring it in once a week, we bring in speakers. Experts on gang violence. We connect them in the community, based on organizations, so that they can mentor, talk to these kids, find out what their home environment is, and then that's the kind of thing that we can do.

Mr. BLACKMAN. One of the lessons I believe we might learn from the war is that showing not just the bombs falling, but the victims of the shooting that hasn't been seen today. I will need to emphasize as to the increase, the interest is, insofar as we can encourage it. An awareness of what the victims suffer rather than on the bombing and the shootings. All that encourages in the media and in the schools to try to get people to (inaudible) in after the tour. To the extent we can do that, I think people will be less problematic to engage in private gangs. Thank you.

Mr. RUSH. Thank you, Mr. Chairman. I think it's my round of questioning, and I just have one comment. First of all, I want to thank all the witnesses, and I want to thank all the students for their involvement. I think you should give yourselves a round of applause.

There is one area, of course, I wanted to get into, and that is what I'm really concerned about, and I want us to think about it as we proceed with additional Chairman hearings in the field, and that is: The increasing incidences of violence committed—violence committed by one young female as opposed to males. And maybe we can get into that real soon at some additional point in time.

But again, these questions, we asked you, of course, for your participation, and your presence, Mr. Chairman, is really, really well noted, and it's very, very important to us as a community, and also as a citizen of this Nation, and I want to thank you for bringing this subcommittee to Simeon High School and for taking the time out. You didn't have to do this, but you did anyhow, and we certainly appreciate you for your commitment and for your leadership on this issue that faces our Nation. Again, thank you so much.

Mr. UPTON. Thank you. Let me say in conclusion, and in addition to chairing this subcommittee, I serve on the Educational Committee. And I've been to a school every week, whether it would be an elementary school, like I did at St. Mary's last Friday, or a high school class, or a college university. And often, I can tell as I walked in the door, the quality instruction, the students are receiving good teachers. And I got to say, looking through these questions that were presented today, I know this is a great school. And I'm really proud of each of you in the issues that you have to be a wonderful American. And that's the appreciation that Bobby Rush is the leader for. He doesn't shine just today, he shines every day.

He is an active participant in every issue that we have had over the years, and he has had over the years in our subcommittee, and it was a great joy that we can pick a date out. He actually picked the day and the site. And for me to come, and Mr. Shimkus's participation, as well. This is an issue of concern, finally a Member of Congress puts in an appearance. And as you look to the future, I can assure you that we're getting paid to work shoulder to shoulder on the issues that confront our Nation every which way.

Thank you all, and thank you panelists for being here and sharing your testimony and taking the opportunity to be a part of this record. We look forward to interacting with you. And with that, the hearing is adjourned.

[Whereupon, the subcommittee was adjourned.]

[Additional material submitted for the record follows:]

PREPARED STATEMENT OF THE AMERICAN ACADEMY OF PEDIATRICS

The American Academy of Pediatrics, representing 60,000 pediatricians, regrets that an AAP member could not testify in person, but we would like to submit this statement for the record. We appreciate your leadership and interest in how the media, particularly television, impacts the health and behavior of children and adolescents.

Our three main points are:

- Although there are potential benefits from viewing some television shows, many negative health effects in children can also result. These include aggressive behavior, desensitization to violence, nightmares and fear of being harmed. By knowing how television affects children, we can make TV viewing for children less harmful and still enjoyable.
- It is not violence itself but the context in which it is portrayed that can make the difference between learning about violence and learning to be violent. Studies show that the more realistically violence is portrayed, the greater the likelihood that it will be tolerated and learned.
- Parents, health professionals, the entertainment industry and policymakers all have critical roles in discussing and addressing television violence.

The Academy recognizes exposure to violence in media, including television, movies, music, and video games, as a significant risk to the health of children and adolescents. The young people of this country drink in media all day, every day. What would we do if we discovered that the water our children drink was full of factors toxic to their physical and mental health? The question for consumers and producers of media is simple: in what kind of environment do we want our children to grow up?

Over the last 20 years, the AAP has expressed its concerns about the amount of time children and adolescents spend viewing television and the content of what they view. Although there are potential benefits from viewing some television shows, such as the promotion of positive aspects of social behavior (e.g., sharing, manners, cooperation), many negative health effects also can result. Extensive research evidence indicates that media violence can contribute to aggressive behavior, desensitization to violence, nightmares and fear of being harmed. Children and adolescents are particularly vulnerable to the messages conveyed through television, which influence their perceptions and behaviors. Television can inform, entertain and teach us. However, some of what television teaches may not be what parents want their children to learn. TV programs and commercials often show violence, alcohol or drug use, and sexual content that are not suitable for children or teenagers. By knowing how television affects children, we can make TV viewing for children less harmful and still enjoyable.

IMPACT OF MEDIA ON HEALTH AND BEHAVIOR OF CHILDREN

Starting from when we are very young, we get the majority of our information from media. While media offers us, including children, many opportunities to learn and to be entertained, how people interpret media images and media messages also can be a contributing factor to a variety of public health concerns. Among children and adolescents, research shows that key areas of concern are:

- Aggressive behavior and violence; desensitization to violence, both public and personal
- Substance abuse and use
- Nutrition, obesity and dieting
- Sexuality, body image and self-concept
- Advertising, marketing and consumerism

This morning we are focusing specifically on television violence. Research in a variety of circumstances and settings has shown that the strongest single correlate with violent behavior in young people is previous exposure to violence. Before age 8, children cannot discriminate between real life and fantasy. On-screen violence is as real to them as violence that they witness at home or in their community. From childhood's magical thinking and impulsive behavior, adolescents must develop abstract thought and social controls to prepare them to deal with adult realities. If this development process occurs in a violent environment, it can become distorted. Media, with which children spend more time than with parents or teachers, have great potential for shaping the hearts, minds, and behaviors of America's young people, and we need to take this potential very seriously.

Entertainment violence is not the sole factor contributing to youth aggression, anti-social attitudes and violence. Family breakdown, peer influences, the availability of weapons, and numerous other factors may all play a part. But entertainment violence, including television, does contribute. The media are an area of clear risk that we, as a compassionate society, can address.

VIOLENCE IN CONTEXT

It is not violence itself but the context in which it is portrayed that can make the difference between learning about violence and learning to be violent. Serious explorations of violence in plays like *Macbeth* and films like *Saving Private Ryan* treat violence as what it is—a human behavior that causes suffering, loss and sadness to victims and perpetrators. In this context, viewers learn the danger and harm of violence by vicariously experiencing its outcomes. Unfortunately, most entertainment violence is used for immediate visceral thrills without portraying any human cost. Sophisticated special effects, with increasingly graphic depictions of mayhem, make virtual violence more believable and appealing. Studies show that the more realistically violence is portrayed, the greater the likelihood that it will be tolerated and learned.

Children learn the ways of the world by observing and imitating—they cannot help but be influenced by media. Exposure to media violence results in an increased acceptance of violence as an appropriate means of conflict resolution. Media exaggerate the prevalence of violence in the world and offer strong motivation to protect oneself by carrying a weapon and being more aggressive. Perhaps the most insidious and potent effect of media violence is that it desensitizes viewers to "real life" violence and to the harm caused its victims. The more realistic, comic, or enjoyable the media violence, the greater the desensitization. Given what we know through research, why is violence marketed to children? To quote Dr. David Walsh, author of *Selling out America's Children,* "Violent entertainment is aimed at children because it is profitable. Questions of right or wrong, beneficial or harmful are not considered. The only question is 'Will it sell?'"

As medical professionals, pediatricians want parents and the television industry to understand that TV programs can have powerful positive and negative effects on child health. They can be used to teach wonderful, enlightening and entertaining lessons to children but also can show graphically violent, cruel, and terrifying images that can lead to aggressive behavior in some children and nightmares, fearfulness or other emotional disturbances in others.

RECOMMENDATIONS

Free speech and open discussion of society's concerns protect our liberty. We do not want censorship, which is both unconstitutional and ultimately unsuccessful in a free society. However, we need to help children make the best media choices, just as we try to do with the food they eat. Parents, health professionals, policymakers and the entertainment industry each bear some responsibility. For example, parents should set content and time limits on media use, monitor and discuss the media their children consume, and take televisions out of the children's bedrooms. Pediatricians should alert and educate parents when positive media opportunities arise, either educational or informational. Policymakers need to enforce and in some cases, strengthen laws and regulations that protect children as media consumers. They should also increase the funding available for media research. The AAP endorses legislation in the Senate, "Children and Media Research Advancement Act," to fund and generate more research on how media impacts children. We should also support media education programs in American schools that have been demonstrated to be effective.

ROLE OF TELEVISION INDUSTRY

Lastly, the entertainment industry needs to acknowledge that it is an important and powerful force in American society, one that affects all of us in many ways. Too often scientific research on the effects of media on children and adolescents is ignored or denied by some in the entertainment industry. Yet the leading medical groups in this country, including the American Academy of Pediatrics, American Medical Association, American Psychological Association and the American Academy of Child and Adolescent Health, all echo the same conclusion. Based on decades of research, viewing entertainment violence can lead to aggressive attitudes, values and behavior, particularly in children. It is time for everyone in the entertainment industry to join us in protecting and promoting the health of our children.

Many in the industry are parents, grandparents, aunts or uncles themselves. As individuals they care deeply about children and youth. We are simply asking them to take their personal values into the workplace as they pursue their business. Though many producers and consumers of entertainment media express helplessness to change the flood of violence, this problem will only be solved through the efforts of media producers and media consumers who decide to reject violent media. As the entertainment audience we must focus on what we want our young people to learn and how we want them to behave. To do so, we must support positive entertainment products and reject negative and dangerous media products, including violent TV programming.

If the television industry accepts our invitation, we can start talking about reasonable and practical solutions. The AAP and its members have been working on many fronts to help parents and children glean the best from unending media exposure. The AAP launched its Media Matters campaign (www.aap.org/advocacy/mediamatters.htm) seven years ago to help pediatricians, other health professionals, parents and children become more knowledgeable about the impact that media messages can have on children's health behaviors. Public education brochures on the media have been developed and distributed, including one that explains how the various ratings systems work. In addition, the Academy established a Media Resource Team (www.aap.org/mrt) in 1994 to work with the entertainment industry in providing the latest and most accurate information relating to the health and well being of infants, children, adolescents and young adults.

Until more research is done about the effects of TV on very young children, the American Academy of Pediatrics does not recommend television for children younger than 2 years of age. During this time, children need good, positive interaction with other children and adults to develop good language and social skills. Learning to talk and play with others is far more important than watching television. For older children, the AAP recommends no more than 1 to 2 hours per day of quality screen time.

The AAP has supported federal legislation and regulation when necessary over the years to help address TV violence. We supported the v-chip to help parents control which programs their children see and negotiated with the industry to revise their TV ratings system. However, we still have a lot to work on. Parents don't know much about the v-chip and how to use it, nor can they easily decipher the TV ratings system. Many parents find the ratings unreliably low, with an objective parental evaluation finding as much as 50% of television shows rated TV-14 to be inappropriate for their teenagers. The "TV Y7 FV" rating is often thought to mean "family viewing" instead of "fantasy violence" for children age 7 and older. The ratings are determined by industry-sponsored ratings boards or the artists and producers themselves. They are age based, which assumes that all parents agree with the raters about what is appropriate content for their children of specific ages. Furthermore, different ratings systems for each medium (television, movies, music and video games) make the ratings confusing. We have called for simplified, content-based media ratings to help parents guide their children to make healthy media choices. Until we achieve that, the v-chip and current ratings system should be extensively publicized by the industry.

In our "Media Violence" policy statement, we have also urged the industry to:

• Avoid the glamorization of weapon carrying and the normalization of violence as an acceptable means of resolving conflict.
• Eliminate the use of violence in a comic or sexual context or in any other situation in which the violence is amusing, titillating or trivialized.
• Eliminate gratuitous portrayals of interpersonal violence and hateful, racist, misogynistic, or homophobic language or situations unless explicitly portraying how destructive such words and actions can be.

If violence is used, it should be used thoughtfully as serious drama, always showing the hurt and loss suffered by victims and perpetrators.

DIGITAL TELEVISION

The AAP, as part of the Children's Media Policy Coalition, has been urging the Federal Communications Commission (FCC) to adopt new public interest obligations for children's television programming for the transition to digital television. This transition offers the best opportunity to shape how this new technology can serve children. Some of what we have called for includes more educational and informational (E/I) programming for children, consistent icons denoting E/I programs, on-demand ratings to be called up at any time during the program (with a brief explanation as to why for example, a show has a "V for violent" rating), and an open v-chip to accommodate any new ratings systems in addition to the industry's rating system.

CONCLUSION

Ultimately, we are all in this together and we should seek a collective solution. Parents, health professionals, the entertainment industry and policymakers have critical roles in discussing and addressing television violence, particularly when it comes to the health of children and adolescents.

Given the overwhelming body of research indicating the danger posed by media violence to the normal, healthy development of our human resources, we need to focus on nurturing and preserving those resources, our children and our nation's future.

Should you need any additional information, please do not hesitate to contact us at 202-347-8600. Thank you.

Lightning Source UK Ltd.
Milton Keynes UK
19 March 2011

169549UK00001BA/1/P